FIRE

AND

POWER

By William D. Atwill

THE

AMERICAN

SPACE PROGRAM

AS

POSTMODERN

NARRATIVE

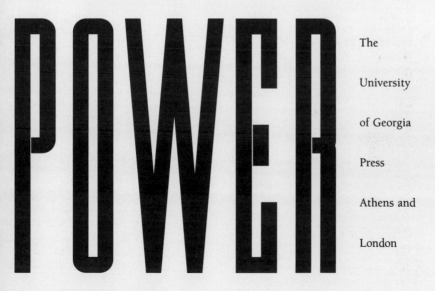

POWER

The

University

of Georgia

Press

Athens and

London

© 1994 by the University of Georgia Press
Athens, Georgia 30602
All rights reserved
Designed by Mary Mendell
Set in Berkeley Medium by Tseng Information Systems
Printed and bound by Maple-Vail Book
Manufacturing Group
The paper in this book meets the guidelines for
permanence and durability of the Committee on
Production Guidelines for Book Longevity of the
Council on Library Resources.
Printed in the United States of America
98 97 96 95 94 C 5 4 3 2 1
Library of Congress Cataloging in Publication Data
Atwill, William D.
Fire and power : the American space program as postmodern
narrative / William D. Atwill.
p. cm.
Includes bibliographical references and index.
ISBN 0-8203-1647-4 (alk. paper)
1. Astronautics—Social aspects—United States. 2. Astronautics—Political
aspects—United States. 3. Literature and technology—United States. 4. American
literature—20th century—History and criticism. 5. United States National
Aeronautics and Space Administration—History.   I. Title.
TL789.8.U5A88   1994
303.48'32—dc20   93-40985
British Library Cataloging in Publication Data available

This book is dedicated to the memory of

Lt. j. g. James R. Atwill, a navy pilot

stationed at Banana River

Naval Air Station,

who in 1943 met and married

May Inman Gray, of Cocoa, Florida.

After the war, they returned to Florida,

raised four children

in the shadow of the U.S. Manned Space Program,

and prepared them for the future.

Thank you for being my parents.

Contents

Acknowledgments   ix

1. Fire and Power: A Narrative
of the Space Age   1

2. Machines for Going Away: Mr.
Sammler and the Labor of Puritanism   25

3. Docile Bodies at Verity Press:
Disciplinary Space in *Rabbit Redux*   45

4. Between a Rock and a Hard Face: Norman
Mailer's *Of a Fire on the Moon*   67

5. Desert Space and the High Frontier:
Tom Wolfe as Text Pilot   91

6. Chemistry and Colonialism Gone Ballistic: Apprehending
the Mass of *Gravity's Rainbow*   117

7. Terror in a Lonely Place: Anomie and
Anomaly in *Ratner's Star*   139

Notes   157

Bibliography   163

Index   169

Acknowledgments

During the time I have worked on and through *Fire and Power,* I have become indebted to many people for their moral and intellectual support. Lou Budd, Frank Lentricchia, Alex Roland, Jane Tompkins, and Marianna Torgovnick of Duke University read early drafts and offered salient criticism.

My good friends at the University of North Carolina at Wilmington have always been generous with their time and insights. Special thanks go to Gil Aegerter, Lindsay Pentolfe-Aegerter, John Clifford, Phil Gerard, Melton McLaurin, Dan Noland, and Lee Schweninger to name but a few. Former and current department chairs JoAnn Seiple and Dick Veit have helped immeasurably by allowing me reduced course loads and favorable teaching schedules.

Carolyn Simmons, dean of the College of Arts and Sciences, was generous with summer research stipends, which not only relieved financial burdens but also signaled her administrative commitment to faculty development.

My thanks to Malcolm Call, Trudie Calvert, and Madelaine Cooke at the University of Georgia Press for their astute judgments.

Above all, heartfelt thanks to my wife, Karen, for her love and support and to my daughter, Elizabeth, joyful child that she is, for keeping me supplied with innumerable works of space art "for my book."

FIRE

AND

POWER

Happy are those ages when the starry sky is the map of all possible paths—ages whose paths are illuminated by the light of stars. Everything in such ages is new and yet familiar, full of adventure and yet their own. The world is wide and yet it is like a home, for the fire that burns in the soul is of the same essential nature as the stars; the world and the self, the light and the fire, are sharply distinct, yet they never become permanent strangers to one another, for fire is the soul of all light and all fire clothes itself in light.

—Georg Lukács, *The Theory of the Novel*

There are ways of getting back, but so complicated, so at the mercy of language that presence back on Earth is only temporary, and never "real" . . . *passages out there are dangerous, chances of falling so shining and deep. . . . Gravity rules all the way out to the cold spheres, there is always the danger of falling.*

—Thomas Pynchon,

Gravity's Rainbow

Fire and Power: A Narrative of the Space Age

I have had the same night-mare for thirty years. Maybe the word *nightmare* is too strong; call it a disturbing dream that recurs at odd intervals, sometimes years apart, sometimes twice in the same week. The basic dream is this: I am standing on a point of land, all gently rolling grass surrounded on three sides by blue ocean. The sky is also blue, dotted here and there with puffy cumulus clouds, and I am looking up in fear. Directly above me, in a flash of fire and sunlit metal, something has exploded. There is no sound, not yet, just the silent arcs of black metal with white tails spinning out behind, falling toward this place where I am standing. It is one of those moments of slow motion, as in an accident you see unfolding but are powerless to move fast enough to prevent. In this case I am paralyzed by the accelerating trajectories of the debris, because even in my dream I know that I cannot run out from under the explosion; any place I run to is as perilous as where I stand. So I stand, heart pounding, sweating, breathing rapidly, waiting to see if I am hit or spared. I awake into that interval of uncertainty where dreams are as true as the bed and walls around me.

Even as I had these dreams I knew their genealogy, though I did not then think of them as Cold War nightmares. As a child growing up among the palmetto scrub and air bases of Florida, I once watched a B-47 bomber blow up in midair less than a mile from the school yard where I was standing. The roaring gray mass of shadow swooping across the field froze our play, froze us not because of the noise or the rushing shadow (we were used to that) but because we were the children of the last war. We knew our aircraft, and we knew this one was too low. The next moment the plane disintegrated in a bright flash, a greasy roil of flame and smoke, a deep, rolling concussion. One wing, on fire along the jagged edge where it was ripped from the fuselage, spiraled like a smoking leaf, falling, falling, drawing out the instant of impact far longer than any equation of height times acceleration might logically derive.

That was October 9, 1957, five days after the Soviet Union had launched *Sputnik,* the orbiting exclamation point to an intercontinental ballistic missile (ICBM) technology that had been escalating since the first German V-2 had landed on London in September 1944. In the paranoia and hysteria following this Soviet space coup, the explosion of one obviously obsolete bomber seemed little more than further confirmation that America was deeply vulnerable. But I had seen it happen, not just read about it in the paper, so I mourned the loss of men and machine because, even at age ten, I understood bombers. Missiles were different, although I had also watched them from the jetty at Canaveral Inlet, three miles from the gantries. My perception of the missile program was that it created giant fireworks. Along with most of the general public, I believed our engineers could barely get a rocket past the launch tower, and when they did, the missile was usually so erratically off course that it had to be blown up by the range officer.

The five years between 1957 and 1962 were the peak years for missile development at Cape Canaveral. In a total of 780 launches (201 in 1960 alone), something was launched on average every two and a half days.[1] I watched countless liquid—and solid—fuel ICBMs spin and veer and then explode above the palmetto dunes of the Cape or out over the blue Atlantic. Those I didn't see personally were played out in black and white on the nightly news, accompanied by Walter Cronkite's lugubrious voiceover. There were successes, finally, including the suborbital and orbital manned missions of Project Mercury, but they seemed almost anomalous alongside the litany of failures and always a little anticlimactic, coming as they usually did after some more spectacular Soviet exploit in space.

In October 1962 the full implication of the strategic power of missiles brought the bombers back to the foreground of my consciousness. During those warm nights of the Cuban Missile Crisis I slept fitfully, hearing even in my sleep the rising whine to full power of multiple jet engines thrusting one B-52 after another into the air as every base in Florida stood at full alert. The sky was full of bombers circling in the stratosphere. At school we learned to "duck and cover" beneath our desks. We rehearsed evacuation routes. Our parents read Pat Frank's *Alas Babylon* and Nevil Shute's *On the Beach*. Even nature reminded us, if we knew where to look, that death came for some from the sky. Above the estuaries there were osprey, pelicans, and other shorebirds with folded wings falling upon fish swimming too close to the surface. After the crisis passed and the air bases came off full alert, there was a residual echo that I would hear off and on for as long as I lived in Florida. Whenever the wind was right (in my memory it is always sometime in March, when orange blossoms scent the air), if I awoke in the night I would register at the edge of my consciousness the engine run-up of B-52s ready on the flight line.

Clearly, my childhood in Florida was punctuated by the aerial and the predacious, and who I am as an adult has a great deal to do with a personal history inextricably linked to the rocket and the world it shaped. This is not to say that all that history was sinister. Gradually, as the United States closed the "missile gap" and began to exceed the Russian space spectaculars, we as a nation began to relax and think not of missiles as weapons but of rockets as transport to the moon and stars. I rode along on the media trajectory of the Manned Space Program throughout the 1960s as, in the collective mind of the nation, Cape Canaveral was transformed from the Joint Long Range Proving Ground for tactical missiles to Spaceport, U.S.A.—Gateway to the Stars.

Over the years, my life has taken me away from central Florida; men were still going to the moon when I last lived in the town of Cape Canaveral. If I thought about the space program at all, it was to believe that the intervening twenty years had reduced its influence in my life by counterbalancing more earthbound cares against my spacebound youth. I had stored all my collective anecdotes almost apolitically, if not ahistorically. Then two things reopened my involvement with the space program. The first was the *Challenger* disaster that cold January day in 1986, when the surreal lotus bloom of seven dead astronauts was replayed endlessly on television until I felt I was seeing, in the networks' nonstop spooling of the explosion, the return of the repressed. The second was the textual power of Walter McDougall's . . . *the Heavens and the Earth: A Political History of the Space Age.* What follows is discursive in every sense of the word, but I don't know any better way to map the contours of the technological enterprise that has become the historical marker of our age, particularly as it intersects with my professional interest in contemporary American literature.

In the national soul-searching that followed the *Challenger* tragedy I found myself revising (literally "seeing again") my own personal narrative of America's ambivalence toward space. Not since Henry Adams's "Dynamo and the Virgin" has a technology's cultural impact been viewed as so nearly Manichaean in its importance.[2] As transport to other planets, rockets may be key to our survival as a species; as supersonic weapon, they represent the delivery system for nuclear devices of total annihilation. Is it any wonder that every dialectical and binary construct from theology to physics finds its way into the literature of rockets? Or even into literature itself, in such works as Thomas Pynchon's brilliant but maddening *Gravity's Rainbow,* which is, among many things, a meditation on the implications of living in a *Raketen-Stadt,* a "Rocket City" of the psyche, a world shaped not by geography and national origin but by the intricately multinational lines of technocracy that emerged after World War II and burgeoned in the Cold War climate of the next two decades.

Add to this ambivalence the very public (televised) history of the space age and you have, perhaps, the best example of Guy Debord's postmodernist "Society of the Spectacle" as well as this century's benign version of Michel Foucault's "spectacle of the scaffold" in the sense that the space program served as a public stage on which a sovereign's power and control were inscribed on the hearts and minds of the assembled through a mediated enactment upon representative individuals. I don't mean to equate televised launches with public executions, which served as terrorizing demands for obedience from the populace, but something closer to the ceremony accompanying the launch of a new ship-of-the-line in previous centuries. That is, the space program was the most effective display of power in this century, a dispersed, nearly invisible coercion of the souls of people by way of a technological display apparently benign in its application. We were thrilled at the technological possibilities of communications satellites, weather satellites, probes to distant planets, and voyages of men to the moon, but all those years of admonition to "watch the skies" hovered at the edge of our consciousness to remind us that more sinister payloads could also be delivered.

Toward this end, President Dwight D. Eisenhower made a masterful decision to create the civilian National Aeronautics and Space Administration (NASA) that projected an image of rocket development and space exploration as open, peaceful, and scientific. In the hands of the Kennedy administration, it guaranteed a public display of power in the most spectacular way. On March 20, 1961, NASA administrator James E. Webb would write in a memo to the president: "The extent to which we are leaders in space science and technology will in large measure determine the extent to which we, as a nation, pioneering on a new frontier, will be in a position to develop the emerging world forces and make it the basis for new concepts and applications in education, communications, and transportation, looking toward viable political, social, and economic systems for nations willing to work with us in the years ahead."[3]

I am hard-pressed to name any other event that has been as media-saturated, institutionally sanctioned, or successfully signified as William James's "moral equivalent of war" as the Manned Space Program. Television brought the spectacle into our living rooms, *Life* magazine offered weekly installments of courage, virtue, and fortitude from both astronauts and their wives. Protestant middle-American values, ever the cultural dominant, were sanctified by the sacrifice of those brave men of the space program. The space race was white, male, and military, if not militant. It was keeping America free by showing the world the technological expertise of democratic values fueled by federal mandate, corporate desire, educational incentive, and military involvement. As Webb knew so well, each success in space was another ideological round fired in the Cold War.[4]

As public spectacle, the moon landings have no rival in all of history precisely because the technology that made the mission possible had already been employed to set up a global electronic communication network of orbiting relay satellites. Michael Smith's fine essay "Selling the Moon" makes the case that NASA's exploits in space were from the very first ripe for televised public consumption.[5] With long countdowns, numerous delays, brief moments of dramatic action, followed by the monotony of jargon-filled communication and "science editors" with scale models, a launch of any duration provided television viewers with more of what Norman Mailer called commercial "vending space" than outer space.[6]

Every product with even the most tenuous link to the space program was sold to the public in a patriotic iconography not seen since World War II. Project Mercury, Project Gemini, Project Apollo—each launch was more spectacular, more record-breaking than the preceding one, until July 20, 1969, when Neil Armstrong stepped onto the moon's surface. After that, boredom, no new stunts. Then in January 1986, the first "ordinary" citizen chosen to go into space, schoolteacher Christa McAuliffe, became a media darling and, seventy-two seconds after launch, a retinal afterimage.

Perhaps because it was not an urgent newsbreak into the regularly televised program, but rather, once again, *the* program, the *Challenger* disaster has come to represent a darker side of the space race, whose ostensibly brightest moment was the *Apollo 11* moon landing. Over the years these culturally shared moments have mixed with so many private but no less powerful moments to form the inner architecture of our own histories. They remain most familiar to us as collective anecdotes made possible by mass communication. Don't we all share a visual point of view of *Apollo 11* and *Challenger* and most other televised events, from sports to terrorism, given to us from the fixed position of the cameras and edited by news programs in such a way that we all feel as if we had been standing together watching the event unfold? Only the most powerfully variant versions of a received narrative are able to defamiliarize one of these public spectacles enough that we can, once again, see that event in all its strange and unique immediacy.

That happened to me when I picked up Walter McDougall's *. . . the Heavens and the Earth: A Political History of the Space Age* because I thought it might add some historical detail to my personal memories of growing up with rockets. The opening paragraph began: "I missed the first moon landing. In July 1969 I had the night shift as chief of artillery fire direction in a particularly nasty jungle base in the III Corps region of South Vietnam. A three- or four-day-old copy of *Stars and Stripes* told us of *Apollo 11*. I do not recall that it made much of an impression on us, except maybe to poke our ready sense of irony."[7]

So public and immediate had the moon landing been in my own sense of history that it never occurred to me that anyone missed it, and, having missed it, that the only impression it might make was that of irony. *Irony*? What was ironic about the moon shot? Did it have something to do with the way those who fought in Vietnam dislocated themselves from "the world," as they called every place other than the war zone? Did the soldiers in Vietnam feel so far removed from what was happening in America and the space program that they might as well have been on the moon? Or was it that McDougall's own artillery fire direction reduced portions of the cartographically unplaceable "III Corps region" to the terrestrial simulacrum of a moonscape? Perhaps it referred to the part of Richard Nixon's speech to the astronauts on the moon where he claimed: "People all over the world . . . join with Americans in recognizing what a feat this is. . . . It inspires us to double our efforts to bring peace and tranquility to earth. For one priceless moment in the whole history of man, all the people on this earth are truly one."[8]

It is fairly certain that no one in McDougall's hot corner of the earth was feeling any excess peace, tranquillity, or brotherhood during that summer of 1969. Or perhaps it was the irony that missiles, after all, were tactically superior extensions of the artillery he was directing and, as such, made the futility of his presence in Vietnam that much more acute.

McDougall's laconic anecdote reminded me that the massive technological spectacle of the Manned Space Program was, on one level, inseparable from the more violent displays of hegemony carried out by military force. That is not a particularly new or startling conjecture in and of itself. But his linkage of the space program to Vietnam is somehow more powerful because it chronicles the displacement from "history" of one man, and by extension thousands of others, unable to bask in the red glare of some benign rocket because they are too busy plotting the last delta-*t* of their own ordnance, or living in fear of the enemy's, in a place as alien and cratered as the moon.

McDougall's preface made me realize how easily I had separated in my own memory the benign history of NASA from the malignant history of Vietnam. But there was something else in the passage, a voice or voices I'd heard before, some intertextuality that recalled the combat narratives of war correspondents such as Richard Tregaskis, Ernie Pyle, or that more famous Ernest— Hemingway. That was it—the voice of Hemingway's narrator of *In Our Time,* obliquely traversing his own parabolic horror of an earlier war. On another frequency it is the voice of industrialization, of Frederick Taylor, of production nonstop and time partitioned into "shifts"; it is the voice of imperialism, remapping and rewriting the history of a place.

Perhaps in this pastiche of narrative voices lies the tension and urgency that have kept the race to the moon and the malaise of Vietnam embedded in the American psyche but somehow separated. If the movement from modernism to postmodernism did indeed accelerate after 1967, then it is little wonder that both the Vietnam War and the Manned Space Program became something of a generic "no-man's land" for writers attempting to map their narrative terrain.[9]

Because I had witnessed much of the space program in a way that conflated media coverage of it with my own eyewitness account, I became intrigued with discovering how it was being written not just into our political history but also into our literary history. A large body of work is already in place, actively tracing the contours of the Vietnam experience on the American landscape, but surprisingly little work has been done until recently on the space program as parallel narrative of that decade.[10]

What interests me is the difficulty so many writers had telling this story of a technocratic enterprise simultaneously central and antithetical to the time and place that produced it. In a sense, the space program had already become what we call postmodern. The rise of television as a global force was linked to the space program's ability to orbit geosynchronous relay satellites, and, just as the astronauts were almost never out of contact with ground control, no writer living through those times could avoid the media saturation of the launches. The print and electronic news networks anticipated each launch weeks in advance, celebrated the space exploits almost moment by moment as they occurred, and then reexamined them after splashdown.

Because it was event as fait accompli, built up and played out on television before anyone could write about it at length, the same difficulties, albeit more benign, confront the chroniclers of the space program that troubled the war correspondents in Vietnam. Both are writing to audiences that believe they already know the authenticity of the events televised by the networks and photojournalistically displayed in magazines such as *Life, Newsweek,* and *Time.* Both Vietnam and the space program were events that unfolded in one of those synchronic interstitial zones where no new terms were in place to discuss them, although Fredric Jameson's introduction to postmodernism establishes a metaphoric linkage:

> This latest mutation in space—postmodern hyperspace—has finally succeeded in transcending the capacities of the individual human body to locate itself, to organize its immediate surroundings perceptually, and cognitively to map its positions in a mappable external world. And . . . this alarming disjunction point between the body and its built environment— which is to the initial bewilderment of the older modernism as the velocities of space craft are to those of the automobile—can itself stand as the symbol and analogue of that even sharper dilemma which is the incapacity of our minds, at least at present, to map the great global multinational and decentered communications network in which we find ourselves caught as individual subjects.[11]

Jameson's characteristics of postmodernism seem particularly applicable to the organizational structure and design of the policy makers involved in putting a man in space and then on the moon. In their comparative inarticulateness about the uniqueness of the

lunar landing, the very "flatness" of response on the part of astronauts and engineers, there is the postmodern tendency to erode
subjectivity, emotion, or feeling from narrative. The thoroughly rehearsed and simulated scenarios of the mission create a tone of
laconic depthlessness in the verbal exchanges between astronauts
and mission control. There is about the space program an efface-
ment of hierarchy that not only breaks down distinctions of bureaucratic delineation but also erases some of the lines between high
culture and mass culture.

Because we see them as a pastiche of earlier images of personal
heroism, we cannot imbue the astronauts with those characteristics of solitary genius or grand pioneering design that would make
them some version of Wallace Stevens's single artificer of the world
whose voice makes the sky "acutest at its vanishing." And finally,
there is a very real need on the part of NASA to engineer all surprise out of the project of going to the moon. The technological
enterprise is so large and contingent that every stage must be rou-
tinized into a myriad of small, interconnected functions. So vast
is this dispersion of tasks that the space program and its systems
analysis managerial style have a pervasive sense of grand design
that, at times, seems to border on paranoia.[12] Conspiracy theories
of the time ranged from the grand hoax in the desert Southwest
that NASA merely staged the landing to blaming crop failures on
changing weather patterns disturbed by meddling in space.

The lunar landings crossed all boundaries of human experience from the mathematical precision of vector analysis to the
ethereal realm of superstition. Chroniclers struggled for metaphors
of diachrony: Devonian evolution, cathedral building, Columbus
and the New World, railroads and the American West. For some the
exploration of space was a wonderful, upbeat story in an otherwise
chaotic decade. For others, it was a senseless waste of technology,
money, and priorities. For a few—and these are the chroniclers
who interest me—the Manned Space Program was the most visible

and outward sign of a radical shift in the culture that fostered it. For these writers the effort to put a man on the moon represented the ideological condition of its time and place.

Politically, it was just what the epigram from James Webb's memo to President John F. Kennedy said it was, the crux move in a Cold War struggle for the hearts, minds, and political allegiances of Third World countries, hence inseparable from the United States's military intentions in Southeast Asia. Psychologically, the moon mission reopened a "frontier" of the American mindscape, if not landscape, that Frederick Jackson Turner proclaimed closed in 1893. Virtually every text locates the space program as an extension of the myth of the West. The narrative of a pioneer voyage into space was, in the parlance of newsprint journalism, a "brightener"—one of those good news, upbeat stories that could be placed on page 1 to counteract the depressing litany of violence and death unfolding in urban ghettos, Vietnam, and the Third World in general. As televised spectacle it fulfilled what Colette Brooks perceives as the powerful cultural impulses "channeled" by the concept of an open frontier: "the thirst for novelty, the expectations inherent in the fresh start, the sensation of mobility itself . . . epitomized in the annihilation of time and space."[13] If Ralph Waldo Emerson believed that the altered point of view afforded by a coach ride through one's own town turned a street into a puppet show, then consider how the electronic transport of television has made the world that street and every event on it a spectacle.

Economically, the space program marked the largest and most ambitiously unique public works project of all time, actively involving in a new way the industrial sector, academic research, and the military in a display of technological power that has been the paradigm for institutional research ever since. Aesthetically, it presented one of those inescapably sublime moments in human history, a spectacular mechanical Prometheus carrying the fire to new worlds. NASA itself made the greatest effort at historical quotation by appropriating Greek and Roman mythology. Manned space projects named Mercury, Gemini, and Apollo and rocket boosters named Atlas, Aegena, and Saturn were attempts to ennoble this latest effort through allusions to the heroic rhetoric of previous civilizations with global designs. But aesthetically, the Manned Space Program was vexing because it came across as rational, calculated, sterile, passionless, routine, and rehearsed.

The nature of the space program demanded minute planning—the spatialization of time into discrete tasks—and the men (there were no women) chosen for this journey were men with high boredom thresholds, men capable of endless rehearsals of routine tasks. They weren't the adventurers of earlier decades, they were "company men" of a corporate government. They were hard to write about in and of themselves; their hardware was more exciting.

In those narratives of the Space Age whose critical reception or mass appeal has invested them with near-canonical authority— Saul Bellow's *Mr. Sammler's Planet* (1970), John Updike's *Rabbit Redux* (1971), Norman Mailer's *Of a Fire on the Moon* (1970), Tom Wolfe's *The Right Stuff* (1979), Thomas Pynchon's *Gravity's Rainbow* (1973), and in another way, Don DeLillo's *Ratner's Star* (1976)— one of the common concerns is an acute awareness of the troubled status of "history" even while it is being written into the collective memory of a culture.[14] That is, these texts are not so much chronicling the Manned Space Program as they are writing about how the sense of an "actual" history of that massive Cold War enterprise was represented by the media of the time. At its most grandiose, the "conquest of space" was depicted as part of a grand evolutionary process by Wernher Von Braun and, by extension, part of the master narrative of manifest destiny that informed the American experience.[15] The lunar missions even inspired John Dos Passos to make the incredibly redemptive claim that landing on the moon was "the day man proved his mastery of matter, the day he wiped out the unhappy prospects of Hiroshima."[16]

This sense of mission, this errand in the wilderness of space, was portrayed by the media as altruistic, almost self-sacrificial, with no hint of all the exploitative possibilities available. Perhaps this was a common issue throughout the 1970s because various Vietnam War narratives critique the same propagandistic efforts in the early years of that conflict. At any rate, when one sits down to read *Mr. Sammler's Planet, Rabbit Redux, Of a Fire on the Moon, The Right Stuff, Gravity's Rainbow,* and *Ratner's Star,* one cannot help noticing how nearly every page attempts in one way or another to call into question the received narrative that has been put in place by a comparatively uncritical news media. The authors of these texts are aware of the mass-imaging power of the media even at the moment it is occurring, and one of the pleasures of rereading Bellow, Updike, Mailer, et al. is discovering that they are offering, in the quotidian lives of their characters, a sense of the potential cost of such an undertaking as going to the moon even at the moment the enterprise had its strongest hold on the national psyche. Their own sense of where they were located in the matrix of time and place, however, led these authors to structure their narratives in varying ways.

The novelists of social realism such as Bellow and Updike do not seem to question the ability of language to represent the overwhelming complexity of technological America and its mass culture. They focus instead on the inability of individuals like Artur Sammler and Harry Angstrom to assimilate the rapid change taking place around them. At that moment near the end of the 1960s some could still believe that comprehension of the velocity could be managed from the proper point of view.

The metadiscursive texts of Tom Wolfe and Norman Mailer, which were creating a space for themselves at this same time, were not so confident. Neither fiction nor history by any conventional definition, the literary journalism they were writing was heavily concerned with the problem of expressing the inexpressible. Their texts are anxious about the limitations of language, claiming that technological subjects cannot be rendered comprehensible to those not part of the discipline, then contradicting that claim by creating a style, structure, and syntax that do represent it.

The postmodernist projects of Pynchon and DeLillo seek to trace some parabolic trajectory that allows for the multiple possibilities of meaning in words by representing a nonlinear, non-euclidean world in a textual structure equally as adrift from the formulaic constraints of traditional narrative.

All of these roughly coordinate texts call into question the ever-changing status of the novel. The issues involved are the theoretical status of narrative, the implication that has for "literary" narratives, and in some sense the way certain narratives are, simultaneously, keepers of the status quo and arbiters of change at a moment when the "end" of so many things seems at hand. Mailer seems to speak for all the writers trying to map the landscape of their culture when he bemoans "a tendency of American society to alter more rapidly than the ability of its artists to record that change. . . . The American phenomena had to do with the very rate of acceleration. It was as if everything changed ten times as fast in America, and this made for extraordinary difficulty in creating a literature."[17]

All of them, Bellow, Updike, Mailer, Wolfe, Pynchon, and DeLillo, try to trace out genealogies that work backward from the illusion of a continuous, stable, received history of the space program circa 1969 to various moments of discontinuity and find there suppressed or silent parallel narratives that have been disfranchised in some way by the force of the dominant text. Time and again, in the work of these writers, that moment of discontinuity is linked to changes in technology and balances of power wrought by the effects of World War II.

The development of the rocket is only the most obvious example of the consequences of that war, but its design and Manichaean function allow it to serve as the representative metonymy of our time. Perhaps the impulse that is driving me to reexamine these texts now—more than twenty years after the last astronauts traveled to the moon, fifty years after the first V-2 was developed, and five hundred years after Columbus—is similar to the need these writers had to reexamine the cost of the Space Age on the collective psyche of a culture. In their narratives, the expense of constructing rockets that threatened destruction as well as offered deliverance is measured by more than hours worked and money spent. The bureaucratic structure that oversees the projects, the way resources are prioritized and allocated, the division of labor, and the manipulation of public perceptions are all shown to operate at the expense of other social priorities.

In *Mr. Sammler's Planet,* Saul Bellow interrogates a number of contemporary texts that popularized the notion of technology's modifying influence of human behavior. Max Weber's social history of the Puritan ethic and the rise of bureaucracy is important to Bellow's novel, as are more current texts such as Victor Ferkiss's *Technological Man* (1969) and Hannah Arendt's *Eichmann in Jerusalem* (1967).

Hannah Arendt's attempt to understand how such "ordinary" little men as Adolf Eichmann could be responsible for the genocidal horror of the Holocaust leads her to coin the phrase "the banality of Evil." Victor Ferkiss transposes the term in *Technological Man* to stand in for the utter ordinariness that he sees in the astronauts and the entire space program. Bellow uses this celebration of banality as a disjuncture between the old values of Artur Sammler—which will not allow for the trivialization of either science or evil—and the values of the contemporary world in which he is living. Employing H. G. Wells's aphorism "Science is the mind of the Race," Bellow constructs a novel of social realism that examines the implications of British imperialism, German Weimar intellectualism and Nazism, American technocracy, and the precarious state of modern Israel, to examine the consequences of twentieth-century experiments in techno-social engineering.

For John Updike, in *Rabbit Redux,* the astronauts on their way to the moon, and even their technocratic support staff, signify an actual and symbolic distance separating the interests of corporate government and the vast heterogeneous population of America. The subject of the novel is midcentury America's inability to understand its own pluralist dynamic. The white working-class values of Harry Angstrom are brought into conflict with generational, economic, ethnic, and racial histories that have been distorted or suppressed by hegemonic institutions like the one where he is employed, Verity Press. The stark technological contrast between televised coverage of the lunar landing and his own encapsulated space at the linotype machine pales before the difference in what he believes is history and what the black radical Vietnam veteran, Skeeter, teaches him of Frederick Douglass and African-American history. The narratives Skeeter, Stavros, and Jill bring to Angstrom open up to him the possibility that more than one version of world events might exist.

For Mailer the genealogy of Project Apollo has followed a trajectory of power that begins with "the subtle elaboration of state capitalism," of large corporations that he feels belong to the government (though the opposite is more likely), seeking to "transform life into a huge commodity."[18] Fueled by its own self-validating epistemology, the triumph of corporate rationality has resulted in the grand, irrational engineering feat of putting a man on the moon. In *Of a Fire on the Moon* he sets up the dialectic of romanticism and the sublime against the technologic banality of corporate America. For Mailer, what is threatening about the rise of the technocratic state is its interwoven power/knowledge network that is so effective that it can appropriate any and every symbol of a more poetic and, in a sense, irrational, discourse and employ those symbols to consolidate its power further. The moon, the names of Greek gods, the Bible, the American myth, all are useful to the corporate state. The real insidiousness is that power is not repression, constraint, or prohibition, but rather something irretrievably linked to knowledge that on one hand enables power and on the other allows power to create new objects of knowledge.[19]

In Tom Wolfe's *The Right Stuff*, on the surface the most straight-forward and unproblematic book about the first years of the Manned Space Program, there seems at first little evidence of this inverted millenarianism. *The Right Stuff* is Wolfe's project to recover the history of the X-series rocketplane tests at Edwards Air Force Base and the direction they were taking the space program in the years following World War II. After the Soviets launched *Sputnik* and forced the United States into a catch-up mode, the quick-fix solution of launching a man into space atop an ICBM effectively terminated the space plane project with its test pilot heroes, including Colonel Chuck Yeager. In its place was Project Mercury, a mission that planned to have men functioning as test subjects for scientists and engineers, not as test pilots. This new approach to putting a man into space was completely consistent with what Wolfe perceived to be the emerging ideology of the postwar Eisenhower era, a time that Vincent Leitch refers to as

> an urgent historical narrative about the dispossession of rug-ged individualists in favor of outer-directed conformists who were manipulated by government bureaucracies and corpo-rations and stripped of political and psychological potency. Mass man was puny, weak, dependent, repressed, controlled, and absurd. The subduers of man were corporate capital-ism, big government, mass advertising, rampant technology, rigid social conventions, coopted science, and total adminis-tration—all of which tamed the opposition and fostered docile conformity.[20]

The Right Stuff is the story of how Project Mercury was re-inscribed into the American western myth of personal heroism and solo combat by what Wolfe calls the "Victorian Gent," the un-adversarial mass media of the 1950s, and how this media-generated perception made an ideological space for the astronauts themselves to take control of Project Mercury.

Thomas Pynchon, writing *Gravity's Rainbow* very much in

the moment of the moon landings (1969–72), maps out a zone of history that, among many other subjects, explores the failings of colonialism by the Germans in Southwest Africa, the Puritans in America, the Russians in Kirghizstan, the Dutch in Mauritius, and the English everywhere. Like Mailer, Pynchon sees this capitalist expansion of commodity markets as blurring lines of territory and influence. World War II becomes the focal point of all the insanity—an hourglass of failed colonialism funneling through the venturi of Germany at the close of the war to drive the world into the rocket state of multinational capitalism and nuclear paranoia.

In *Ratner's Star* (1976) Don DeLillo internalizes the effect of the space program and charts a course through late Space Age technocratic America by leading the reader into an unmappable cycloidal structure of interconnecting and radically disconnecting language systems. The languages of math, bureaucratic acronyms, physics, anthropology, economics, banality, and babble are employed to create a world so cataloged and available to description that the only terrifying possibility left is not anomie but anomaly.

My desire to reexplore the various ways novelists have written a variant version of our public history of the Manned Space Program into our literary history has provided me an opportunity to examine not just the technocratic narrative that science presents but also a culture in transition from a modernist project that sought to discover an interior, individual unity within a chaotic outer world, to a culture moving toward a postmodernist "scattering" (to borrow back a term borrowed by physics) wherein the fragmented subject never knows exactly where it is standing. As Bellow, Updike, Wolfe, Mailer, Pynchon, and DeLillo repeatedly demonstrate, this need to place oneself in the grid and thereby become oriented to the infrastructure supporting NASA is not only impossible, it may be undesirable.

After all, there seems no personal or unique style to any of the workers at NASA; they are all, as Mailer asserts, "subtly proud of their ability to serve interchangeably for one another . . . they had depersonalized themselves."[21] To write about this project one has to speak in categories of dimension both imaginary and actual. For Wolfe it is a metaphoric pyramid of expertise and luck that test pilots with the "right stuff" ascended in their careers; for DeLillo it is a cycloidal structure that cannot be cognitively mapped; for Mailer it is the Vehicle Assembly Building at Cape Canaveral, an actual structure "of breadths and vertigos and volumes of open space. . . . One did not always know whether one was on a floor, a platform, a bridge, a fixed or impermanent part of this huge shifting ironwork of girders and suspended walkways."[22]

NASA's absolute reliance on computers and a globally decentered data-link communication network to constantly monitor its spacecraft makes it the most visible evidence of an emerging American postmodern culture engaged in Third World colonization through the commodification of information. It required very real grid space across the world to link up its communication network—conjuring up the most bizarre disjunctive architecture—concrete block tracking stations with huge parabolic dish antennae and barbed-wire perimeter carved out of the poverty of some remote jungle. Capital and labor were dispersed throughout thousands of subcontractors located in virtually every geographic region of the United States and even some foreign countries. As a result, NASA spoke a language dominated by categories of space rather than of time and memory.

This emphasis on spatiality is most accessible to us in its architectural representation of individual and clustered space in the form of buildings and entire cities. The space program is constructing the transport of the future and planning the self-contained communities of tomorrow within a post–World War II infrastructure dominated by crumbling urban landscapes. The image of the city that emerges in the literary narratives of the late 1960s and early 1970s is one of decay, displacement, disorientation, disconnection, and despair. Perhaps it is the inescapable contrast of the vast emptiness of interstellar space with the prescribed enclosure of the cityscape that prompts them, but the influential narratives under discussion here all emphasize a culture living inharmoniously with its constructed environment.

Reexamining the ways this cross section of writers felt compelled to incorporate the Manned Space Program into their own literary agendas during the decade of the 1970s reminds me again of the power of literary texts to be the narrative of the quotidian in the midst of more visible "history." As novelists and literary journalists, Bellow, Updike, Mailer, Wolfe, Pynchon, and DeLillo have all achieved a certain cultural status that extends beyond their professional craft, so their concerns about articulating the reactions to spectacular events through the lives of their characters indicates more than a passing unease with the facile narratives propagated by the news media. Their function is to be interpreters of that experience, to be critics as it were, of the noble, the misdirected, the wasteful, and so on, not with an eye toward representing the chronological events as any less momentous than they were but as vastly more intertwined and compromised by the circumstances of cultural production.

We that are of purer fire

Imitate the Starry Choir,

Who in their nightly watchful Spheres,

Lead in swift round the Months and Years,

The Sounds and Seas with all their finny drove

Now to the Moon in wavering Morris move,

—Milton, *Comus*

2

Machines for Going Away: Mr. Sammler and the Labor of Puritanism

Late one night in the spring of 1969 I drove from Tampa across the darkened peninsula of Florida to meet some friends at the Jetties, a long granite breakwater across the inlet from the launch sites at Cape Canaveral. It must have been for the *Apollo 10* launch. I remember the smell of orange blossoms hanging heavy over Merritt Island and, in the distance, pencil beams of searchlights visible to the north. It would be inaccurate to say that the launch didn't really matter, but it was more the carnival atmosphere of the campers gathered among the stunted scrub oak and palmettos that drew us.

We had grown up with rockets. We watched them from school yards; we had seen the Disney animation, listened to Walter Cronkite. Our fathers worked there. For us, manned launches meant tourists, motor homes, home movies of history in the making for the middle class. They were also magnets for crazies. The lunatic fringe loved space; it fed their paranoia. Disheveled old men in rusting cars, only their eyes shining like new metal, could collect a crowd with their conspiracies. Typical monologues went something like this:

"Range officers suddenly got three more blips on the screen, just shadowing that rocket right up out of the atmosphere. . . . They been watching us for years . . . they check out every shot. . . . Got bases built on the dark side of the moon and underwater between here and Bermuda. . . . Why you think so many planes and boats disappear out there?"

Tonight was different. The man was middle-aged, his hair trim around the ears, face lean and tan, neatly dressed in dark slacks and muted yellow sport shirt, clear eyes, no reek of alcohol. He spoke with quiet assurance to a blond girl and her boyfriend, who looked like locals, surfers waiting for sunrise. The rapt intensity of the girl and boy, their unwavering attention to his words, drew others. His voice never rose above a conversational tone as he talked about MENSA and its election, that it was in contact with the extraterrestrials, that a new order was coming. He was good; he had the stoned and the gullible in his grip, mouth-breathing in slack-jawed attention.

"Watch the northwestern quadrant of the sky just before dawn," he told them. Told us. "You'll see the stars over there start to disappear. That's where they'll be stationed, out beyond the ionosphere. If you know where to look and there's no moon or no clouds to blur it, you can always find them where the sky is blank."

That was all he would say. He knew the power of concision. We walked away laughing. An hour or so later, around 3:00 A.M., a cluster of people looking inland toward Titusville began to murmur and point. Beginning at the horizon and moving slowly up the sky, stars were disappearing. First they went fuzzy, then they faded, then they vanished altogether. The hair on the back of my neck prickled. For the next two hours I believed in the millennium. Then, a slow gray dawning, a red sky, revealed a bank of clouds moving in from the northwest—a cold front. There was more of meteorology than MENSA to this mystery. If space was going to come to us it wasn't going to happen today. We'd been astounded by someone who knew something about weather forecasting and gullibility. So we, a flotsam of counterculture washed up among gleaming machinery of middle America, turned our eyes north and also waited as the monological voice of Mission Control counted down the seconds. "Five . . . Four . . . Three . . . Two . . . One . . . we have ignition." A tremendous roll of smoke, fire, then a slow silver ascent. "Liftoff." *Apollo 10* was on its way to the moon. Another rational spectacle of power and engineering had been launched in the name of a mythological god.

I tell this anecdote because it reminds me of a scene in *Mr. Sammler's Planet* in which the wastrel nephew of Artur Sammler is stumped by the *New York Times* crossword puzzle. He cannot come up with a name for an old English dance that begins with "m." Sammler, without hesitation, suggests "morrice," then quotes the line from Milton's *Comus,* which in the lunar-landing year of 1969 had a unique context. The world that Wallace and Artur inhabit is, in Sammler's view (and it seems to be Bellow's as well), filled with "A thousand fantasies / . . . Of calling shapes and beck'ning shadows dire" (206–7) that threaten it. Unlike the Lady in the masque, for whom "These thoughts may startle well, but not astound / The virtuous mind, that ever walks attended / By a strong siding champion—Conscience" (210–12), the danger lies precisely in the present culture's ability to be "astounded." Stanley Fish's gloss on Milton's distinction between "startle" and "astound" as the basis of the definition of virtue holds for Bellow's moral vision as well:

> Milton conceives of virtue as a state of inner composure, a moral readiness that cannot be shaken, even by something totally unexpected. The virtuous mind may be surprised (startled) at a possibility hitherto unknown . . . without losing its balance; it will absorb and assimilate new facts and situations, not disintegrate before them. On the other hand, a mind that is astounded has allowed the weight of external pressures to paralyze it and rout it; it has become the plaything of circumstances instead of their master.[1]

Bellow's Artur Sammler is a virtuous man in a world where the "labor of Puritanism was now ending," and for him the mind of his culture has become the plaything of circumstance.[2] The cities of the north, those "dark Satanic mills" of Augustine and Blake, whose technological progress had created the best and worst of the twentieth century, are now, in Sammler's mind, under the tropical sway of exotic and uninhibited influences. Sammler has, we are told, "seen the world collapse once" and believes it might again. He is a survivor of the Nazi death camps, a Polish Jew left for dead outside Cracow. Rescued from a displaced persons camp and brought to New York by his physician-nephew, Sammler bears only one physical scar, his "damaged left eye," which "seemed to turn in another direction" (31). One looks to science, the other to religion, but it is impossible to say which. Even the grand technical enterprise of going to the moon is lost on Sammler in this fecund libidinal spring. He cannot say whether spaceflight is just another example of "Machines for going away" like the cars leaving Manhattan, or whether it fulfills some innate need of the soul.

In this narrative of the Space Age Bellow attempts to locate the enterprise in the multiple meanings of "flight." The connotation of flight as "a running away from" is just as present (if not more so) as the sense of flight as "soaring free," or transcending. In both senses Bellow wishes to explore the implications of living without limitations, of humanity breaking free of its asymmetrical parabola of life on earth. But there is an inherent paradox to the contemplation of human flight; to be able to fly free of the bonds of earth into the limitless expanses of sky and space, humans must live confined, must engineer their own enclosure, must work in disciplined concert.

The bifurcated space created by Sammler's double vision is Bellow's device for interrogating what the modern Western world had become in the light of H. G. Wells's proposition that "science is the mind of the race." For Sammler (and for Bellow, who corresponded with Wells before his death) Wells becomes the representative of all that has gone awry in this century. He is Wells the "guesser of genius" who was writing about going to the moon in 1900, Wells whose "Marxism for the great public made him a millionaire," Wells the scientific utopian whose Cosmopolis project failed although the scientific principles underpinning the Nazi horror nearly succeeded. Bellow has created a trajectory for Sammler's life that takes him from childhood in pre–World War I Poland, to London between the wars, to the death camps, and finally to New York after the war. Cracow, London, and New York, the movement is from rich central European culture before World War I, to the last days of English cultural and technological imperialism, to the present site of geopolitical power. New York City in 1969 does not appear to Sammler any more stable than his former residences. Viewed through Sammler's divergent eyes, the illusion of unified dimension created by the mind's need to resolve two different perspectives of the same object is not possible. The present vision of America in the Space Age is one of disintegration. The New York City in which Bellow places him is a city where communications at ground level are literally and figuratively breaking down: "Most outdoor telephones were smashed, crippled. They were urinals, also. New York was getting worse than Naples or Salonika. It was like an Asian, an African town, from this standpoint. . . . You opened an opulent door into degradation, from hypercivilized Byzantine luxury straight into the state of nature, the barbarous world of color erupting from beneath" (7).

But aerially it is a world connected by television antennae, "whiplike, graceful thrilling metal dendrites drawing images from the air, bringing brotherhood, communion to immured apartment people." The world of "light and shadow" that Sammler inhabits has become, simultaneously, a world of global access and of enclosures. The previously bordered world of discrete political, historical, psychological, architectural, and gendered spaces is still outwardly in place but tremendously fluid. Though he does not name it as such, Bellow has given a working description of postmodern space.

As an Anglophilic Polish Jew living in Manhattan, Sammler is about four standard deviations beyond the normal border dweller. He lives in a room provided by his dead wife's niece. He is supported financially by his own nephew. Sammler floats free of job, home, or nationality, his days, at age seventy-four, primarily spent in interior spaces. He awakes in his room at six, rides buses to the library to study Meister Eckhardt, visits his nephew in the hospital, rides more buses. He is residual rather than vestigial, but his individuality is precarious at his age in an environment of mass values. When crossing streets in traffic or crossing ethics with nearly everyone in the novel, "he didn't in fact appear to know his age, or at what point of life he stood. . . . They might run him over, but he could not help his style of striding blind" (6).

The structure of *Mr. Sammler's Planet* seems, like its protagonist, anxious, unhappy with the stylistic experimentation of the times, and content with residual literary values. For Bellow the form of the novel remains stable even if its subject matter does not. He works out of a social realist tradition modified somewhat by modernism but on the whole still grounded in nineteenth-century aesthetics. *Mr. Sammler's Planet* uses a third-person limited point of view and moves linearly (except for flashbacks) through a long weekend in the life of Artur Sammler. Little physical action occurs; Bellow is not particularly concerned with innovation. Earl Rovit even asserts that "the typical Bellow plot is rarely more than a device to bring his protagonist and his reader into a heightened emotional awareness of the thin sliver of freedom that life permits to consciousness. . . . One can readily imagine Bellow under different circumstances being perfectly comfortable as an eighteenth-century essayist . . . slightly contemptuous of such errant frivolities as fiction."[3]

This is a novel that pretty much conforms to Benjamin DeMott's assessment at the time that "conservatives are locked in the habit of fitting every observation of behavior or feeling into a grid of Cultural Decline."[4] If Norman Mailer is, as he likes to label himself, something of a radical conservative, then Bellow is something of a conservative liberal. *Mr. Sammler's Planet* is, for the most part, a jeremiad against modernism's socially alienating pull and postmodernism's historical depthlessness, but Bellow has Sammler hold out some possibility for resolving the apocalyptic spiral of astounding cultural decline. Sammler sees an alternative to fleeing a planet rendered uninhabitable by technology and the quest for individuated "wholeness," but it requires a return to "virtue," a reconciliation to an almost Puritan asceticism whose discipline follows not from the absence of any clear knowledge of God's will but from the absence of any knowable God. This is no longer the virtue of Milton's Lady in "Comus," certain of her election, but more the antinomian Milton of *Samson Agonistes,* nearly "eyeless in Gaza," trying to judge his own frailties, cowardice, and ignoble motives.

At the moment novelist Bellow was writing *Mr. Sammler's Planet* he was also, as Professor Bellow, actively involved in the work of the Committee on Social Thought at the University of Chicago. This group, formed to "unify recent discoveries in the arts and sciences," no doubt appealed to Bellow's formal training as an anthropologist and sociologist.[5] The theoretical implications of interplanetary travel for society had been a subject of considerable inquiry throughout the 1960s and had been discussed in other sources besides scientific journals and the popular press. Donald Menzel's "Space—The New Frontier" appeared in *PMLA* in 1962, and Bellow's Committee on Social Thought colleague Hannah Arendt published "Man's Conquest of Space" in the *American Scholar* in 1963.[6] By the late 1960s the early enthusiasm had been tempered somewhat by the civil strife at home and the quagmire of Vietnam abroad. The riots at the Chicago Democratic Convention and the circus trial of the "Chicago Seven" provided Bellow with ample close-hand models of "the charm, the ebullient glamour, the almost unbearable agitation that came from being able to describe oneself as a twentieth-century American." With few exceptions, the characters in *Mr. Sammler's Planet* are a parade of all the ills modern society can create—"mankind's own passion simultaneously being mankind's great spectacle, a thing of deep and strange participation" (73).

The central action in the novel grows out of an incident in which Artur Sammler watches a well-dressed black pickpocket working a bus in Manhattan. Whether Bellow might have thought of him as such in 1970, this nameless but exquisitely tailored predator of New York's transit system is thoroughly postmodern. He wears the uniform of corporate power, a tailored suit, expensive topcoat, and designer sunglasses, so he can steal from similarly dressed citizens without attracting notice. He has created his own economy in the congestion and confusion of commuting. He is flourishing precisely because the city is "dis-integrating." When the thief accosts Sammler in the vacant lobby of Sammler's apartment building and, instead of uttering threats, pulls out not a pistol but his own large penis as a symbol of authority and intimidation, Sammler's fears of cultural barbarism seem complete.

Afterward, upstairs, unharmed but shaken, Sammler discovers a manuscript on his bed, *The Future of the Moon,* by a Hindu biophysicist named V. Govinda Lal. The manuscript, "written in formal Edwardian pedantic Hindu English," has been more or less stolen by his daughter for him to use in his work on H. G. Wells. Over the course of the next two days, Sammler will be forced to negotiate the manuscript's return to its rightful owner while attending to his dying nephew and benefactor, Dr. Elya Gruner. A steady succession of degenerate relatives whose lives and intellectual concerns mirror the historical moment complicate Sammler's efforts.

The preceding paragraphs give structural priority to the brief incident of potential violence between the well-dressed young thief and the aging Sammler in part because they dramatize the rupture Bellow seems most concerned with in the culture of the time. He examines also the pain and idiosyncrasies of two generations of Jews scarred by Nazi atrocities and then afforded some measure of wealth and comfort in America, but it is a more nonsectarian issue that troubles this novel. What informs *Mr. Sammler's Planet* with its peculiar terror is Bellow's apparent pessimism toward any future that places its faith in the power of technique. For Sammler, New York is a profoundly insecure place, powerless to correct the breakdown of transportation and communication grids so vital to its existence. Indeed, it is the power of technique that has threatened its own stability through the unique ability of modern man to link up all the diverse cultures and remote places of the earth and move between them with ease.

In a manner similar to Thomas Pynchon's in *Gravity's Rainbow,* Bellow examines the way colonialism imports into the imperial nation beliefs and practices that will undercut the power of that culture even as it is exporting its technologically superior vision. Sammler, with his differing eyes—the damaged left one that sees only "light and shadow" and the discerning right "trained by the best writers to divert . . . with perceptions"—can profess to his nephew's daughter that he still believes Wells's maxim that "science is the mind of the race" because "it's a better thing to emphasize than other collective facts, like disease or sin. And when I see the wing of a jet plane I don't only see metal, but metal tempered by the agreement of many minds which know the pressure and velocity and weight, calculating on their slide rules whether they are Hindus or Chinamen or from the Congo or Brazil" (30).

That is, one of Sammler's eyes (the one blind to all but light and shadow?) finds in the shaping power of science and engineering a monologic discourse that erases the borders of geographic, racial, and ethnic origin. But the "agreement of pressure and velocity and weight" is not always employed for humanitarian aims, nor is it always sufficient to keep things airborne. Within the brief narrative of his own life he has seen Germans strike Poland on the power of aerodynamic lift, Allied bombers pulverize Germany but spare the concentration camps, Israeli jets blast Syrian tanks, a commercial airline crash kill Ussher Arkin, and Wallace Gruner crack up a private plane. The conquest of flight up to the point of the conquest of space has been closely linked to the conquest of nations. Sammler is understandably ambivalent about the future.

So, from another view, when he is not gazing at the engineering marvels of his time but instead observing from a swaying midtown bus what seems to him to be the moral chaos and decline of the most technologically advanced culture in all of history, Sammler is less charitable:

> Dark romanticism now took hold. As old at least as the strange Orientalism of the Knights Templar, and since then filled up with Lady Stanhopes, Baudelaires, de Nervals, Stevensons, and Gauguins—those South-loving barbarians. . . . Such crazy fervor! And now all the racism, all the strange erotic persuasions, the tourism and local color, the exotics of it had broken up but the mental masses, inheriting everything in a debased state, had formed an idea of the corrupting disease of being white and of the healing power of black. (33)

Men are going to the moon while civilization disintegrates around them; that is the crux of Sammler's anger and despair. In his old age, he has become tacitly racist and quietly misogynist. He has lived the folly of the "Cosmopolis" project put forth by Wells, nearly died at the hands of the Nazis' attempt to engineer a society, and has no patience for the hedonism of modern America. As one who had been a survivor of (as distinguished from a victim of) so much of twentieth-century history, Sammler has a peculiar sensitivity to the power of historical representation. Bellow laces his main character's consciousness with an awareness of the world as mediated by modern communication technology:

> Sammler followed these jet phenomena in the *Times,* and in the women's magazines sent by Angela herself. . . . Thus Sammler knew, through many rapid changes, Warhol, Baby Jane Holzer while she lasted, the Living Theater . . . Dionysus '69, copulation on the stage, the philosophy of the Beatles. (31)

> From the start of the [Six-Day War] crisis, he could not sit in New York reading the world press. . . . He refused to stay in Manhattan watching television. (142)

> These are the people who set the terms, who make up the discourse, and then history follows their words. Think of the wars and revolutions we have been scribbled into. (212–13)

Sammler even attempted once to counteract this distortion by visiting Israel as a correspondent during the 1967 Six-Day War, flying to Tel Aviv because he could not sit in New York and read press releases about yet another threat to Jewish survival. But even being present at the site of conflict cannot unmediate it. The unreality of modern travel—hop on a jet for a few hours, then into a hired car and out of town to the war—makes the distant battle that he witnesses, "as in Vista-Vision," a mere spectacle, "bombs . . . spilling from planes as remote as insects. . . . Tiny war sounds" (164).

Later, in the company of a Jesuit in Vietnam battle fatigues who is neither chaplain nor military officer but, like Sammler, there to "cover" the war for a midwestern newspaper, he is allowed a close-up view of Israel's aerial ferocity: "Father Newell seemed to know a lot about gun calibers, armor thickness, ranges. In a lowered voice, out of respect for the Israelis who denied its use, he identified the napalm. . . . It was a real war. These Jews were tough" (251).

As a correspondent for *Newsday,* Bellow traveled to Israel to cover the Six-Day War. Everywhere the collision (and collusion) of religion and science must have been obvious to him. Israel's aerial superiority with its massive firepower neutralized the numerical advantage of Arab ground forces. The American-made weaponry— F-4 Phantoms carrying five-hundred-pound bombs, air-to-ground missiles, and napalm—was identical to what was being used in Vietnam at the same time.

This oblique reference to Vietnam by way of the peripateticism of a fatigue-clad Jesuit is Bellow's only acknowledgment of the other big story on the nightly news in both the real and fictional settings of Mr. Sammler's world. The early reception of the novel by critics who disliked the reactionary point of view fixed on this omission and his attack on the New Left as further evidence of a certain blindness in Bellow's moral vision.[7] He has, after all, had Sammler find as "worthless fellows" Theodor Adorno, Herbert Marcuse, and Norman O. Brown, while embracing such "historians of civilization" as Toynbee, Burckhardt, Spengler, Marx, and Weber.

Max Weber is significant because Sammler quotes him: "Specialists without spirit, sensualists without heart, this nullity imagines that it has attained a level of civilization never before achieved" (54). Weber is generally credited with first charting the hierarchical structure of bureaucratization and its capacity for reducing the individual, the charismatic, to routine function.[8] The discipline and rigid pyramidal command structure of corporate systems is preferable in Sammler's mind to "petted intellectuals who attacked it [Western culture] in the name of proletarian revolution, in the name of reason, and in the name of irrationality, in the name of visceral depth, in the name of sex, in the name of perfect instantaneous freedom" (34).

There is room for responsible individual freedom within the "labor of Puritanism," Sammler believes. To blame everything on alienation and insignificance is to trivialize human culpability; it makes even mass murder ordinary, boring, or trite by abolishing individual conscience. When Margotte, Sammler's niece, begins to analyze Hannah Arendt's phrase "the banality of evil," he lashes out:

This woman professor's enemy is modern civilization itself. She is only using the Germans to attack the twentieth century —to denounce it in terms invented by the Germans. Making use of a tragic history to promote the foolish ideas of Weimar intellectuals. . . .

The Germans had been the giants of this Method in industry and war. To relax from rationality and calculation, machinery, planning, technics, they had romance, mythomania, peculiar aesthetic fanaticism. These too, were like machines. . . . Machines in the sense of being systematic. System demands mediocrity, not greatness. (19)

Professor Arendt is not the only woman to attract Sammler's criticism. In fact, every female character in the novel is found deficient. Sammler bemoans his wife's insistence that they return to Poland with their infant daughter in 1939 to look after financial interests because it cost Antonina her life at the hands of the invading Nazis and warped Shula's personality for life. Margotte Arkin is portrayed as a pseudo-intellectual who "talks junk." His nephew's daughter, Angela Gruner, is coarse and promiscuous, the product of a "bad" education at Sarah Lawrence. It is as if none of the women can function without men to provide for them, correct their stupidity, and generally keep them pointed in the right direction. This attitude is certainly not inconsistent with the personal history of Sammler, product of bourgeois eastern Europe and "old-boy" Oxford network that he is. But the absence of even one sympathetic female character in a novel written during the rise of the women's movement seems more than faithful attention to detail, particularly when factored in with the attack on Hannah Arendt.

Arendt's work is important to Bellow's intent in *Mr. Sammler's Planet*. Her book *The Human Condition* (1958) is another narrative like those of Marcuse and Norman O. Brown which examine the modern human condition in light of rapid technological change.

The Human Condition begins by setting the importance of the recently launched *Sputnik* above anything man has done, including splitting the atom. Because that launch enabled the realization of the Archimedean effort to envision earth from a vantage point distanced from it, that is, from space, it also threatens to diminish the stature of the human condition. To Arendt all scientific endeavors separate us further from natural existence. She pursues this line further in "Man's Conquest of Space" (1963), ending the essay on a note similar to Norman Mailer's concern in *Of a Fire on the Moon*. Arendt, like Mailer, fears that the science and technology that might make the conquest of space possible will so radically displace the familiar grounds of human discourse that "under these circumstances, speech and everyday language would indeed be no longer a meaningful utterance that transcends behavior even if it only expresses it, and it would be much better replaced by the extreme and in itself meaningless formalism of mathematical signs. . . . The stature of man would not simply be lowered by all standards we know of, it would have been destroyed."[9]

The antagonisms, similarities, and complex dialectics of Bellow's and Mailer's literary careers have been summarized nicely in Earl Rovit's "Saul Bellow and Norman Mailer: The Secret Sharers" so I will not rehearse them here.[10] Instead, I want to argue that Mailer is an unacknowledged if not exactly small presence throughout *Mr. Sammler's Planet*. His three-part narrative of the *Apollo 11* moon shot appeared in *Life* magazine during the time Bellow was writing his novel. There is a reference to "all those guys running for mayor like a bunch of lunatics" (122), which, in addition to adding one more piece of social-realist detail to a novel about life in New York City in 1969, indirectly rebukes Mailer's brief public ambitions. Most significant, though, it is Mailer's radical individualist, that fiery seeker of wholeness in a world too governed by system and restraint, that is Bellow's target.

Sammler rails out against the abdication of restraint by mass culture. It is a society that refuses to accept limitation, refuses to settle for the disciplined state, and insists instead on the guise of individuality. It is a culture relying on technique, on machinery, to deliver it from the constraints of the ordinary. It is Wallace Gruner in the guise of José Ortega y Gasset's mass man who no longer knows the difference between nature and human arrangements, thinking the "cheap commodities—water, electricity, subways, hot dogs—are like air, sunshine, and leaves on the trees" (244). The people Sammler sees at bus stops have all adopted romantic disguises, the dress and mannerisms of Eastern mystics, cowboys, Indians, and the like, but never the uniform of the businessman, the cleric, or the soldier, never the representatives of the collective institutions that keep things running.

Viewed from this perspective, the implications of traveling to the moon have sinister ramifications for Sammler that are diametrically opposed to those of Mailer's Aquarius. Instead of being the triumph of collective corporate enterprise, the disciplined cooperation of mass man, the impulse to travel in space for Sammler is the latest and most exorbitant example of willful flight from the pressing exigencies of this planet. Hence the $20 billion enterprise of going to the moon by the end of the decade becomes the grandest whimsy of an unrestrained culture.

It is particularly significant that the most eloquent defense of this enterprise should be by Dr. V. Govinda Lal, a Hindu Indian who speaks a very precise, formal colonial English to Sammler, whose own Oxonian English belies his ethnicity. He is genuinely fond of Dr. Lal because he is intellectually engaged, but he resents his dark appeal to daughter Shula and niece Margotte. Here Sammler's misogyny connects with his persistent Eurocentrism and his linkage of cultural disintegration to the licentiousness of Asian, Mediterranean, African, and South American mores now openly embraced by his society. Sammler feels that both women are sexually attracted to Dr. Lal because he is a scientific incarnation of the exotic Eastern mystic. His message of transport and transcendence represents the appropriation by science of religion's consolatory space, and a popularizer like Lal carries the day like a television evangelist.

The traditional image of the merger of science and religion— "the good physician"—has died with Elya Gruner, died, in fact, before him. Throughout the novel Sammler has struggled to return to the bedside of the dying Dr. Gruner, but his errand has taken him into the modern wilderness of the city. Gruner has died by the time he returns to the hospital. After threatening to make a scene in the corridor, he is taken down through a labyrinth of passage-ways, ramps, tunnels, and laboratories to the morgue. Alone at last with Gruner's body, "deprived of one more thing, stripped of one more creature," Sammler eulogizes Gruner:

> At his best this man was much kinder than at my very best I have ever been or could ever be. He was aware that he must meet, and he did meet—through all the confusion and de-graded clowning of this life through which we are speeding— he did meet the terms of his contract. The term which, in his inmost heart, each man knows. As I know mine. As all know. For that is the truth of it—that we all know, God, that we know, that we know, we know, we know. (313)

The voice speaking is Sammler, but it is Sammler the reader of Meister Eckhardt, a thirteenth-century cleric whose asceticism counseled a spirituality based on discipline and discomfort. By stripping away all the things of this world, or having them stripped away by circumstance as has been the case for Sammler, the soul is opened to God's consolation. Even as he reads Eckhardt, Samm-ler "could not say that he literally believed what he was reading" (253–54), but he knows that he cares to read nothing else.

With Elya Gruner dead, the state of modern religion and phi-losophy in the hands of "a bunch of worthless fellows," and Artur

Sammler himself in decline, the world is left at its best to the likes of V. Govinda Lal and Dr. Cosbie, a skillful surgeon but otherwise a red-faced southern ex-football star, and the astronauts themselves. They are the new specialists, the products of a culture that has looked to technique to fill the empty spaces of the human heart.

Bellow believes that writers have the ability to enact social change, and for him, *Mr. Sammler's Planet* is an act of radical politics that grows out of his belief that "radical criticism requires knowledge, not posture, not slogans, not rant. . . . True radicalism requires homework—thought."[11] The Space Age is premature, Bellow seems to be saying in 1970. This sentiment hardly places him philosophically out of step with most of the nonscientific writers analyzing the space program. He has bought into the standard clichés about the inarticulateness and banality of astronauts whom the media tout as modern heroes. Like so many others, he knows that what is achievable technically, through cooperation among specialists, is not transferable to the sort of social engineering necessary to save a world that he believes has taken the wrong path. Too much has yet to be done on this earth before we set out for other worlds. Grand as the enterprise of going to the moon is, it diverts attention, expertise, and initiative away from global problems. It is, in a sense, a waste of human potential. In the words of Sammler: "I suppose we must jump off, because it is our human fate to do so. If it were a rational matter, then it would be rational to have justice on this planet first. Then, when we had an earth of saints, and our hearts were set upon the moon, we could get in our machines and rise up" (237).

And that, finally, is what *Mr. Sammler's Planet* tries to be, a conservative, thoughtful, rational examination of what changes of heart are necessary to achieve justice on this planet before setting off for others. Like its author and its central character, the novel claims to eschew slogans, posturing, and rant and instead grounds itself in thought, discipline, and the acceptance of limitations. That the only people who have ever occupied this privileged space of rationality are middle-aged white men of western European descent seems lost on Bellow and Sammler alike. Eckhardt, Schopenhauer, Toynbee, Burckhardt, Spengler, Marx, Weber, Wells—the canon they compose keeps Sammler's feet bound to this earth.

At least one moment of passage, one it will

hurt to lose, ought to be found

for every street now indif-

ferently gray with com-

merce, with war, with

repression . . . find-

ing it, learning to cherish

what was lost, mightn't we find

some way back?—Thomas Pynchon,

Gravity's Rainbow

3

Docile Bodies at Verity Press: Disciplinary
Space in *Rabbit Redux*

Rabbit Redux is, among other things, a novel about power—the power of authority, the power of language, the power of the past, and the power of inertia to constrain individuals within a culturally determined trajectory. The "re-turning" or sense of being "led back" implied in the title speaks to Harry Angstrom's inability to break free of the mass and inertia that exert such a strong gravitational pull on his life, the lives of the other residents of Brewer, Pennsylvania, and by extension, all who reside within the boundaries of America. The time is summer 1969, and Harry Angstrom at thirty-six is ten years older if not much wiser than the man who heeded the imperative of *Rabbit, Run* and attempted to flee the constricting life of the Eisenhower era. Now he has settled for the uneasy economy of sexual fidelity, family responsibility, and hourly wage employment required of him if he is to live more or less anonymously, if not harmoniously, in urban America.

Harry Angstrom is a seven-dollar-an-hour linotype operator for Verity Press, a small operation that "lives on order forms, tickets to fundraising events, political posters in the fall, high-school yearbooks in the spring, throwaway fliers for the supermarkets, junk mail sales announcements," and that publishes *The Brewer Vat,* a weekly newspaper.[1] He has moved from the declining community

of Mt. Judge, where his aging parents live, to an aluminum clap-
boarded development called Penn Villas on a street misnomered
Vista Crescent, a place of "prairie sadness, a barren sky raked by
slender aerials" (60). Astronauts are on their way to the moon, his
son wants to see *2001: A Space Odyssey,* and his wife is having an
affair with a Toyota salesman. Just as Rabbit has begun to become
a docile traveler of the American Way, the signs disappear and the
road splits.

Like Bellow, Updike uses the traditional economy of the social-
realist novel to create a stable structure, an illusion of order, on
which to plot out *Rabbit Redux.* The focus is a four-month span
in the life of one individual, with the linear sequence of events
dramatized against a background of shared history accessible to all
who would have been reading the novel when it was first published
in 1971.

The novel begins on the afternoon of July 16, 1969—the day
Apollo 11 began its journey to the moon—with the workers of
Verity Press emerging from the dim interior of their work space into
the harsh glare of sunlight and heat in downtown Brewer, Pennsylvania. The scene is visually coordinate with the barren landscape
that Updike can reasonably assume most readers will remember of
the first black and white pictures of the moon landing. The workers
"wince beneath a brilliance like a frozen explosion" in an area
of arrested urban renewal, "a desolate openness, weedy and rub-
bled . . . exposing church facades never seen from a distance" (3).
The choice of simile is not without its own special visual allusion to
another technology of the Space Age: the frozen instant of nuclear
detonation, an aerial blast reducing all, especially the facade of religion, to rubble and desolation. The two new technologies of World
War II, rockets and atomic bombs, have combined into a single
weapon system.

For Harry Angstrom, standing on the sidewalk with his father,
adjusting to the sunlight, this is the last moment of stability in a
life that he quite literally believed to be settled in the same way that

time and gravity work on any object of measurable mass. His father will tell him that he is being cuckolded, and from there the domestic scenarios of denial, investigation, confrontation, and separation will play themselves out. His wife, Janice, will leave him and, in the space cleared by that departure, people will appear from outside his insular world, people whose ideologies are sufficiently at variance with each other to create a microcosm of the culture at that moment—at least the culture as it appeared to John Updike.

The social issues of a country split by racial inequality, sexual exploitation, Vietnam, a counterculture, and attitudes toward technology are all represented by characters in the novel. *Rabbit Redux* chronicles a nation divided by its faith in emerging technocracy and the ideological exploitation of space and its unwillingness or inability to deal with a work force destabilized by industrial obsolescence.

Structurally, *Rabbit Redux* is divided into four sections: "Mom/ Pop/Moon," "Jill," "Skeeter," and "Mim." Each section covers roughly a month of the four-month time frame of the novel and foregrounds the character or characters named in the title. Each section also begins with a piece of dialogue from the transcripts of either the American *Apollo 11* mission or the Russian *Soyuz 5* mission, dialogue that reveals a domestic and sexual subtext. Hovering as they do outside the orbit of the primary text, these epigraphs function much the same way the entire space race does for the characters in the novel. That is, the technology of space is remote to them even when it endeavors to place itself within the vernacular of their day-to-day experience.

The relationship of Colonel Shatalov's high-orbit link-up—*"It took me quite a while to find you, but now I've got you"*—to Harry Angstrom's anesthetized response to both his wife's departure and the moon landing—"I know it's happened, but I don't feel anything yet" (100)—is ironic bracketing of the first order. Shatalov's words compress Angstrom's actions of the last decade; they place this sequel to *Rabbit, Run* at that moment when Rabbit feels safely enclosed within the life he has settled for since his return from his pursuit of transcendence. He moves from enclosure to enclosure, from work space to bar, from bar to bus, from bus to home, in a routine designed by the exigencies of making a living. His is an insular world cracked here and there by news broadcasts from outside but on the whole hollowing itself out from within.

Updike's power in the first section is to take the event the media has heralded as "the greatest week in history" and reveal the paucity of response it creates in the lives of people constrained by their own problems. In Rabbit's case, even the departure of Janice, his wife, cannot shake him out of his inertia at first. He is too locked into the inexorable decline he sees around him. Like Artur Sammler, Harry Angstrom reads a social text of death, disease, and dissent. His mother is dying of Parkinson's disease, his father is withering, the inner city is decaying, too many Negroes are riding the buses, spoiled rich kids are tearing up homes in Connecticut, and Rabbit, at thirty-six, "knows less than when he started . . . knows how little he'll always know" (22). As *Apollo 11* flies through nothingness to an empty moon and back, Rabbit sinks into his own emptiness.

Updike has positioned his narrative at that moment when the popular press was representing the technological achievement of putting a man on the moon as a triumph of both social and scientific effort. Everywhere Rabbit goes, the bar after work, his home, his mother's bedroom, a television is broadcasting the event in the background. Across a "sky poisoned by radio waves" his world is linked to an event unavailable except through the mediation of electronics, yet he is asked to feel a part of the grand drama: "The six o'clock news is all about space, all about emptiness: some bald man plays with little toys to show the docking and undocking maneuvers, and then a panel talks about the significance of this for the next five hundred years. They keep mentioning Columbus but as far as Rabbit can see it's the exact opposite: Columbus flew blind and hit something, these guys see exactly where they're aiming and it's a big round nothing" (22).

This event is a legacy of Kennedy's presidency that has lived on without him at no small cost, a faith in the managerial power and prestige of being the leader in space. What bothers Rabbit about the moon shot is that it is what Jacques Ellul referred to as the triumph of *technique,* the marshaling of "any complex of standardized means for attaining a predetermined result."[2] For all avid television watchers of the previous decade, the engineering marvel had been endlessly rehearsed by personalities as diverse as Walt Disney and CBS science correspondent Jules Bergman. The mystery and intrigue had been so overwhelmed by endless planning that the actual event seems anticlimactic to Rabbit.

As part of this triumph of technique NASA's ingenious plan to decenter and subcontract all its services and hardware assured that most communities could, in some small way, point to their own contribution to the lunar landing effort and thus see this enterprise as necessary to their own local economy as well as to national prestige. In *Rabbit Redux,* Updike seeks to dramatize what was not so visible—the toll that the space program and an escalated Vietnam War had taken on domestic programs designed to aid disfranchised minorities. President Lyndon B. Johnson's "War on Poverty" had been defeated before it began, and the growing unpopularity of U.S. involvement in Southeast Asia made its expense doubly galling. LBJ did not run for reelection and Richard Nixon led the Republicans back to power in time to bask in the triumph of *Apollo 11.*

By depicting Brewer, Pennsylvania, as a former steel town crippled once by cutbacks in that industry, Updike contrasts the diversified infrastructure of the Space Age with the decay of a single-market economy. As the opening scene establishes, the inner city is in bad shape, and various support services are endangered as well. It is a tense time locally, and nightly television broadcasts fluctuate between a relentless narrative of national prosperity built on massive government contracts for NASA or the military and an endless litany of civil unrest. Even in the face of the local decline, the blue-collar segment of the society still retains a nationalistic pride. Harry Angstrom's vision of his father standing at the bus stop after work is a wonderful compression of this sentiment. Earl Angstrom is one of the "little men" who believed that the Democrats had watched out for him and who now sees himself abandoned by the Nixon Republicans: "Pop stands whittled by the great American glare, squinting in the manna of blessings that come down from the government, shuffling from side to side in nervous happiness that his day's work is done, that a beer is inside him, that Armstrong is above him, that the U.S. is the crown and stupefaction of human history. Like a piece of grit in the launching pad he has done his part" (11).

This belief in being part of an American enterprise greater than himself reassures and confuses Harry Angstrom. He desperately wants to believe in some grand and noble mission but cannot seem to find any of that in a project that launches men into vast emptiness toward a lifeless moon. He has placed an American flag decal in the back window of his Ford Falcon as a statement to all those factions who seem bent on destroying his "garden" (21).

To emphasize some of this tension and uncertainty, Updike develops at length the work space that occupies most of Rabbit's day. The day after the *Apollo 11* launch, he is sitting at his linotype machine, setting a story about a local company that built an electronic component for the *Apollo 11* mission. Updike has set up a key juxtaposition early on with this passage. Not only does he go into great detail to describe the operation of the linotype, "a temperamental thousand-parted survival from the golden age of machinery," but he also reproduces the boldface, two-column measure of the print complete with spatial juggling, reset lines, and the jargon of typesetting. For the reader, it is one of those moments when sign and signifier are arbitrary and at some distance. Though he does not show the slugged plates as Rabbit would be reading them, letters reversed, upside down, right to left, Updike does emphasize the irretrievable consequences of mistakes literally set in cooling lead:

> When Brewerites this Sunday gaze up at the moon,
> it may look a little different to them.
> Why?
> Because there's going to be a little bit of Brewer on
> No. Widow. He tries to take it back but the line is too tight to close so he settles for the widow.
> it.
> Zigzag Electronic Products Inc., of Seventh and
> Locust Streets, City,
> Oops.
> Locust Streets, city, revealed to VAT reporters this
> week that a crucial electronic switching sequence in
> the on-board guidance and nabifation computer was
> the on-board guidance and navigation computer was
> was manufactured by them here, in the plain brick build-
> ing, once the site of Gossamer Hos,irey, that thou-
> ing, once the site of Gossamer Hosiery, that thous-
> ands of Brewer citizens walk unknowingly by each
> day. (28–29)

Although the surface text unfolds something of the small-town civic pride and tortured banality of weekly tabloids, the inclusion of miscast lines and the emphasis on the artisanlike skill and craftsmanship required of the typesetter are also significant. The two completely recast lines are about just those divergences that will eventually affect people like Rabbit. He loses his way in spelling a word that defines finding one's way, but in this context it is a modifier—"on-board guidance and navigation computer"—part of that electronic present that is still too removed from his own life to seem real. And yet the implication that "crucial" components are still produced in places like Brewer and might affect success or failure of this distant enterprise is equally hard to grasp.

The other reset line refrains the tenuousness of industries. The eye reading the boldface type is struck by the repetition of "once the site of, once the site of." Gone is the hosiery mill, with its machine-age equipment, replaced in the same "plain brick building" by sophisticated manufacturing equipment for semiconductor chips. The visible architecture of a structure can no longer be a reliable gauge of its interior space. And the linotype that Harry operates is closer to the vanished hosiery mill than the world of Zigzag Electronic Products. His workplace is an endangered space about to be displaced by computerized typesetting and cool offset presses from Philadelphia. Verity Press is about to become a space with no place in it for a white linotype operator with no seniority whose domestic troubles follow him to work.

In *Rabbit Redux* Updike includes five stories being typeset by Angstrom. They are but one of the multiple intertextual devices he employs in the novel. Like the epigraphs and the passages from black history texts, the stories from *The Brewer Vat* offer another version of Updike's America. The news is a place where things happen, a place with a life its own, coordinate but elsewhere, even when the events narrated involve Rabbit, who is dialectically in the position of reading the text and setting the type at nearly the same moment, while having in his memory another version of the same event. This semantic sense that "these things happen all the time in the papers," that "things that threaten . . . like riots and welfare have jumped into the newspapers out of nowhere," as if the news were a place somewhere other than the place Rabbit occupies, but still accessible to it, raises the status of news to a postmodern spatial category.

Thus the silent black and white movements of astronauts on the barroom television, the blaring glitz of Hollywood game shows, and even the newspaper headline glimpsed from a city bus—"Myboya Martyred"—become at the very least cracks or gaps in the enclosed structure of Rabbit's world. More so with those stories that he sets for the *Vat*. In the old organizational scheme of a newspaper, power, in the sense of what constituted news, moved down through owner/publisher to the editorial offices, then to the news desk and copy editors before being set by the linotypist, who then sent it on to the pressroom, where the ideology of the managers was reproduced and distributed. Rabbit sits at that disjunction between the conceptualization and shaping of texts and the mechanistic mass commodification of that product. His labor is skilled but passive, working as he does between the ideological and stylistic constraints of the authors and the physical constraints of mechanical reproduction. He works docilely to make the text fit the space allocated.

I don't want to appear to be making too much of the work Rabbit does, but Updike has carefully selected this moribund craft out of any number of possibilities for his central character. It is a job that places Rabbit in a subservient, precarious, and highly visible position where his labors are measured and known to those in authority, as well as to the masses. If he does not produce on schedule, the paper cannot be printed on time; if he does his job poorly, the mistakes are indelibly there for all to read; yet if he does his job well, the whole labor becomes invisible and lost, becomes the white space surrounding the blocked boldface of "the news."

This news that is molded and cast for *The Brewer Vat* by Rabbit is one of many interesting discourses in *Rabbit Redux*. The five typeset stories reveal another voice in Brewer. As they appear chronologically the headlines create the following text:

"Brewer Factory Components Headed Toward Moon"
"Widow, Sixty-Seven, Raped and Robbed. Three Black
Youths Held"
"Local Excavations Unearth Antiquities"
"Sentenced For Possession"

"Arson Suspected in Penn Villas Blaze. Out-Of-Stater
Perishes."

The first story, about Brewer's contribution to the lunar landing, is one of those true "brighteners" that newspapers run to balance the depressing (but titillating) accounts of raped widows and
racism. Even the account of archaeologically significant excavation
turns out to be the dubious and layered discovery of a Prohibition-
era speakeasy, the foundation of an inn, "the Goose and Feathers,
where George Washington and his retinue tarried one night on
their way west to suppress the Whiskey Rebellion in 1799," and
some artifacts from Brewer's frontier days as an Indian trading
post (167).

As Updike's manipulation of other texts will bear out later, this
is a carefully chosen collection of moments that, however sanitized,
chronicle other moments of power and domination in the history
of the United States. These stories also historicize the present social
state by calling up antecedents—a counterculture flagrantly dis-
regarding legislation designed to regulate morality, a country still
exploiting indigenous populations, and a government prepared to
use force against its own citizens.

The arson story is even more intertextual. Harry Angstrom
finds himself in the position of perpetrator, mediator, and reader
of his own exploits as he typesets the story of violence and death
involving his own home, but by then he is too disoriented by the
instability of "history" to sense the irony.

As a sequel, *Rabbit Redux* is an interesting literary artifact. It is
still focused on the individual trajectory of Harry Angstrom's life,
but his shift from active participant to passive receptor of what life
offers him shifts with it the significance of external events. Rabbit
is no longer running, so, unlike Sammler's concern with "flight," it
isn't a question of whether he would be running toward something
or simply escaping the enclosure of his life. The world must come
to Rabbit in this novel. And so it does with a grittiness and im-

mediacy that Bellow's Sammler, who essentially floats free of the world of work, could never completely experience.

Besides the print and broadcast media that bring the world to Angstrom, the human dynamics of work and private life bring it. The world that he distrusts in the headlines, on the television screen, and on the bus seats beside him takes shape in the form of people who move into his domestic space after his wife departs. The most important characters are Charlie Stavros, the Greek car salesman who has seduced his wife; Buchanan, a black co-worker who invites him to a nightclub; Jill, the strung-out runaway from a wealthy Connecticut home; and Skeeter, the apocalyptic Vietnam vet whose black militancy attracts as it terrifies Rabbit. Two of them, Buchanan and Stavros, hold jobs and represent segments of the work force. The other two, who have cast off surnames and go by Jill and Skeeter, are polarities of the counterculture so celebrated at the time.

Updike's sympathetic treatment of the conservative position held by Angstrom is one of the more enduring aspects of the novel. Angstrom's responses to events taking place in the world are shaped more by what he sees on the television screen than the commentary that accompanies the scene. His interpretation is parochial and commonsensical from his limited perspective. America is trying to assist other countries that want to become like us, which is what they all really desire, or at least ought to. "Cultural imperialism" is not in Rabbit's vocabulary: "Rabbit is locked into his intuition that to describe any of America's actions as a 'power play' is to miss the point. America is beyond power, it acts as in a dream, as a face of God. Wherever America is, there is freedom, and wherever America is not, madness rules with chains, darkness strangles millions. Beneath her patient bombers, paradise is possible" (47).

The world that comes to Rabbit is earthbound and in flux. In contrast to the settled acceptance of time and inertia in his parents' marriage, the crushing weight of his marriage to Janice is gravity of another kind. Janice's infidelity is not initially an act of sexual revolution or of emerging feminism on her part, but these issues which competed for news space with the technological triumphs of 1969 attach themselves to her actions in her rationalization to Harry. She is working outside the home, exposed to the liberal and libertarian ideas of her co-worker Charlie Stavros. Her life is expanding while Harry's remains sealed off.

Also in this first section, Updike uses Charlie Stavros as Bellow does V. Govinda Lal, as representative of the antitechnological fecundity attributed to those darker regions of the earth incompletely mixed with the colder technocracy of Western civilization. Admittedly, Stavros's occupation is not very high tech—he is a Toyota salesman—but he is lumped into the general category of "spic" by Angstrom, meaning swarthy foreigners of not-quite-white heritage who, in his eyes, "come over here to make a fat buck . . . and then knock the fucking flag" (46). Stavros functions as an articulate foil to Rabbit's jingoistic nationalism and narrow parochial interests: "I just can't get too turned-on about cops bopping hippies on the head and the Pentagon playing cowboys and Indians all over the globe. That's what your little sticker means to me. It means screw the blacks and send the CIA into Greece" (44).

Between Stavros and Angstrom, Updike can rehearse all the conservative and liberal clichés of the time. Foreign policy and civil rights are their primary surface flashpoints, although it is the vast morass of sex and the new morality that pits them against each other. Their conflict is serious and emotionally charged but still contested within the social strictures of the dominant white culture. Violence does not appear to be an option for them.

The second section, "Jill," offers Updike an opportunity to explore the issues of feminism and the sexual revolution through Rabbit's encounter with a stereotypical hippie. A young runaway from an upper-middle-class home in Connecticut, Jill embodies all the traits of indulged rebellion popular with the press at that time. She drives a Porsche (but doesn't know to check the oil), she is strung out on heroin, she is sexually active, she is dependent. Jill is, in her youth and her rhetoric of liberation, about as far from Janice as Rabbit can get.

He is introduced to her in a black jazz club called Jimbo's by his co-worker, the enigmatic Buchanan. As it turns out, Rabbit has been invited to the club by Buchanan to get this underage white girl away from the bar before the vice squad clamps down on the place. So Jill, filled with all the clichés of an untested middle-class counterculture, goes home to Rabbit's unexamined establishment Republicanism.

This second section of *Rabbit Redux* begins with an epigraph lifted from Neil Armstrong's effort to describe the surface of the moon: "It's different but it's very pretty out here." The empty content of that sentence is precisely its appeal. Here is an astronaut conforming to the stereotype, a man narrowly specialized in a vastly complex technical discipline that speaks its own arcane language, who cannot go beyond the level of generality inherent in "different," "very pretty," or "out here." Throughout the "Jill" section, Updike will explore the empty content of jargons made popular by media exposure.

The signal that the rhetoric of NASA has passed with the conclusion of "Mom/Pop/Moon" is the movie marquee in Brewer; Rabbit notices it has changed from *2001* to *True Grit*. In this section the dialects and dialectics of pop psychology, hippies, and the Pentagon will dominate. Janice, in her phone calls that pull Rabbit from his linotype cubicle to the foreman's office, will speak of "valid identity" and "motivation." Jill speaks in many voices, the voice of Connecticut privilege, the voice of drugs, the voice of pop religions—"yoga, psychiatry, zen, plucked from the racks at the Acme." Charlie Stavros and Rabbit will invoke bureaucratic jargon to discuss Janice:

> "You're the one screwing another man's wife. If you want to pull out, pull out. Don't try to commit me to one of your fucking coalition governments."

"Back to that," Stavros says.

"Right. You intervened, not me."

"I didn't intervene, I performed a rescue."

"That's what all us hawks say." He is eager to argue about Vietnam, but Stavros keeps to the less passionate subject. (181)

Vietnam is passionate, but arguing about his wife with his wife's lover isn't. That seems to sum up the key inversion in Harry Angstrom; he can be passionate about the events in the news (except for the sterile field of space), but he is unable to feel as powerfully about the things that happen to him directly. He has occasional outbursts of violence, but on the whole, his summer of discontent is passive—until Labor Day, when he arrives home to find that Skeeter has moved in.

The epigraph for the third section is emblematic: " 'We've been raped, we've been raped!'—BACKGROUND VOICE ABOARD SOYUZ 5." In the case of Skeeter, violence is always about to shift from static to kinetic. The threat he poses is nothing so benign as Bellow's lordly pickpocket preying on the soft underbelly of prosperity but more like that of Nat Turner or any of a number of ill-remembered assassins in school yards armed with assault rifles. He is the agent of violent violation of interior and private space. Skeeter has seen the link between Vietnam and an institutionalized racism that holds no possibility for change in America. He is a figure of such anarchic force that he effectively dissolves the political distinctions between Stavros and Angstrom. They are white. They have jobs. They believe, like the agentless, passive president of twenty years later that "mistakes were made" but that, once identified, those mistakes can be corrected and America set on course again. The trouble is not systemic.

That the inner space of America might be systemically troubled is Updike's riskiest proposition in *Rabbit Redux*. In the character of Skeeter the novel explores the militant separatist position of Stokely Carmichael, Malcolm X, and the Black Panther party by placing them in the context of a suppressed historical narrative running from antebellum days through Frederick Douglass, W. E. B. Du Bois, and Eldridge Cleaver. Skeeter's seminar in black history, held in the living room of Rabbit's white suburban home, becomes Updike's guerrilla theater for the middle-class reader. Extended passages are reprinted from their writings, interspersed with rambling drug-fogged memories of Skeeter's tour of duty in Vietnam and the civil strife on nightly television.

It is television that links and distorts. Repeatedly, Updike introduces what Dilvo Ristoff calls the "teleguided" nature of Harry Angstrom's world by describing the often voiceless and usually misaligned picture on the television screen:

> On the television above the bar men are filing past a casket, but the sound is turned off and Rabbit cannot tell if it is Everett Dirksen's lying-in-state in Washington or Ho Chi Minh's ceremonies in Hanoi. . . .
>
> The funeral . . . vanishes, and flickering in its place are shots of cannons blasting, of trucks moving through the desert, of planes soundlessly batting through the sky, of soldiers waving. He cannot tell if they are Israeli or Egyptian. (236)
>
> Six o'clock news. The pale face caught behind the screen sternly says, unaware that his head, by some imperfection in reception at 26 Vista Crescent, is flattened, and his chin rubbery and long. (273)
>
> Eleven o'clock news. A gauzy-bearded boy, his face pressed so hard against the camera the focus cannot be maintained screams, "Off the pigs! All power to the people!" (275)[3]

Like the picture of the moon landing, which was in its harsh chiaroscuro nothing more than "an abstraction," the news of state funerals, Mideast war, SDS riots in Chicago, or the trial of the Chicago Seven is just more evidence of the world of events turning into news that jumps into the headlines out of nowhere for Rabbit.

As the "Skeeter" section progresses, his control of Rabbit, Jill, and Nelson increases with his craziness. Roles are inverted. Rabbit plays out the part of powerless black male forced to tolerate Jill's sexual submission to Skeeter. They are all held hostage to Skeeter's agenda; his rage and bitterness have made the house on Vista Crescent an encapsulated space orbiting outside the norm of the neighborhood. A collision is inevitable.

That collision takes place one afternoon in October, more than a month after Skeeter moved in. Rabbit, walking home from his bus stop, is stopped by two men, Showalter and Brumbach, who are neighbors. Their message is clear—get rid of Skeeter and straighten up the sexual high jinks with that girl. Showalter, who is in computers, "the hardware end," and whose company is going to "revolutionize business in this town," takes the tactful liberal line. Eddie Brumbach, the wounded Vietnam vet who works on an assembly line, is more direct: "'I earned this face,' he says [referring to the wound], 'I got it over there so I could have a decent life here. . . . After what I seen and done, no wiseass is crowding me in my own neighborhood'" (291).

This is in itself an uneasy alliance of white-collar computer designer and blue-collar mechanical worker. Showalter's technocratic world is in ascendancy, displacing as it grows workers like Brumbach and Angstrom. Under ordinary circumstances their ideologies would have made them friends. But the complicated thrust of circumstances that launched Harry Angstrom into the social void now places him in the position of stubbornly defending all the positions his conservatism would normally have attacked. He cannot conceive how threatening he appears to Brumbach and so fatally mishandles the confrontation.

The next night, while he is spending the evening with Peggy Fosnacht, a divorcee who has just begun a new job as a computer keypunch operator, he is called home to find his house firebombed. Jill is dead, Skeeter is nowhere around. Suddenly, all the violence that seemed compartmentalized in the headlines spills out into his life. He has become the news. What's more, the last story that he will typeset for Verity Press is an account of the crime that has so powerfully disrupted his life:

> **ARSON SUSPECTED IN**
> **PENN VILLAS BLAZE**
> **Out-of-Stater Perishes**
> West Brewer police are still collecting testimony from neighbors in connection with the mysterious fire that destroyed the handsome Penn Villas residence of Mr. and Mrs. Harold Angstrom.
>
> A guest in the home, Mill Jiss
>
> A guest in the home, Miss Jill Pendleton, 18, of Stonington, Connecticut, perished of smoke inhalation and burns. Rescue attempts by valiant firemen were to no avail
>
> A man reported seen in the vicinity of the dwelling, Hubert Johnson last of Plum Street, is being sought for questioning. Mr. Johnson is also known as "Skeeter" and sometimes gives his last name as Farnsworth.
>
> . . . Neighbors are baffled by the event, reporting nothing unusual about the home but the skulking presence of a black man thought (339–40)

The preceding 340 pages of *Rabbit Redux* have told quite a different version of relationships and events leading up to this moment so Updike's inclusion of the *Vat's* version is designed to call into question the reliability of any of the mediated ways we think we know what is happening in our community or the world at large. At this moment, Angstrom is interrupted by Pajesk, his foreman, and told that he is being let go because Verity Press is going offset.

So by the final section of *Rabbit Redux,* the technology of computers, which made work for Zigzag Electronic Products and navigation to the moon possible, which Showalter promised would revolutionize business in Brewer, which provided work for Peggy

Fosnacht, now takes work from Rabbit. His marriage is split, his house is burned, and his job is gone. Harry Angstrom is adrift. He is as removed from the banal epigrammatic exchange between Buzz Aldrin and Neil Armstrong as he is from the moon:

COL. EDWIN E. ALDRIN, JR.: *Now you're clear. Over toward me. Straight down, to your left a little bit. Plenty of room. You're lined up nicely. Toward me a little bit. Down. O.K. Now you're clear. You're catching the first hinge. The what hinge? All right, move. Roll to the left. O.K., now you're clear. You're lined up on the platform. Put your left foot to the right a little bit. O.K., that's good. More left. Good.*

NEIL ARMSTRONG: *O.K., Houston, I'm on the porch.*

The domesticity of this exchange, with its sense of quotidian cooperation and purposeful direction, runs counter to the sheer magnitude of what was transpiring. Armstrong's reference to the last step of the ladder descending to the moon as the "porch" locates the entire enterprise back within the suburban landscape of America, a landscape that Rabbit has just seen destroyed by the unresolved racial and political forces pulling at the country.

This last section, "Mim," completes Updike's exploration of possible responses to the shifting grid of America in the Space Age. It also completes his negative stereotyping of women. Rabbit's invalid mother still controls him through her illness, particularly now that he is living at home again. Janice, Jill, Peggy, and Babe, dependent as they are on abstractions like love and fulfillment, and physical needs like sex and drugs, are no longer in control of their lives. Only Mim, as a prostitute, has made a business of her sexuality. She is, in a sense, the synthesis of sex and technology that has been radically disconnected in everyone's response to change up to that point. By professionally and dispassionately seducing Charlie Stavros, Mim succeeds in placing Janice and Rabbit back in the same orbit. They have, to paraphrase Colonel Shatalov, taken quite a while to find each other, but at the close of the book they have each other once again: "The space they are in, the motel room long and secret as a burrow, becomes all interior space" (352).

Updike shares with Bellow the need to end with some sort of limited affirmation. If the chaos that is piped in over the news channels and evident in the gutted interiors of cities cannot be ignored, it can be meliorated to a degree by the novelist's foundational beliefs. As Rabbit explains to Janice, "Confusion is just a local view of things working out in general" (351). And that, finally, seems to be the central message of *Rabbit Redux*. Men may be going to the moon even as the world seems to be tearing itself apart, but that is not cause for either hope of escape or despair at being left behind, Updike seems to be saying. What is required is a degree of faith that things are "working out in general" and an even more patient exploration of the inner spaces of the quotidian.

They lived, it was evident, with no ordinary opposites in their

mind and brain. On the one hand to dwell in the very

center of technological reality (which is to say

that world where every question must have

answers and procedures, or technique

cannot itself progress) yet to in-

habit—if only in one's dreams—

that other world where death,

metaphysics and the unanswerable

questions of eternity must reside, was to

suggest natures so divided that they could have

been the most miserable and unbalanced of men if

they did not contain in their huge contradictions some

of the profound and accelerating opposites of the

century itself.—Norman Mailer, *Of a Fire on*

the Moon

Yes, the future spoke of a human species

which . . . travel to spectacles to

feel extraordinary sensa-

tions.—Norman Mailer,

Of a Fire on the Moon

4

Between a Rock and a Hard Face:
Norman Mailer's *Of a Fire on the Moon*

The cover of *Life* magazine for August 29, 1969, announces in large letters an article on the *Apollo 11* moon landing, but the photograph that fills the space below the masthead is not a grainy black and white image of the moon or a finely composed color landscape of the technological sublime—Canaveral seascape with Saturn booster—but is, instead, the lined and weathered face of Norman Mailer, the author commissioned by *Life* to write the piece. It is a head-and-shoulders shot, front-on, with a strong light source almost directly overhead and slightly to the left. The chiaroscuro settles the head into the hunched shoulders of Mailer's dark windbreaker, his chin and jawline lost in shadow. The face is in its own way a terrain topographically incomplete—the inverted "vees" of flesh along the cheeks losing ground to gravity, leading into the flared contours of a broad nose that converges in the shadow of dark orbits. The eyes are a priori—we believe in them, though the jutting eyebrows emphasize instead the forehead's creases. Mailer's curly hair is a dark corona against a light shading of whites and grays that suggests cumulus clouds building up at midday for an afternoon storm. His head is centered between the dark and the light. No passion here, the hard face seems to say, just an enfolding intellect.

What is most revealing, though, is the very presence of Mailer as subject of the cover shot—that *Life* has chosen to give primary space to an image of the mediator of this historical moment instead of the event itself—signaling, it would seem, at least an equal status for the narrative text. This is not news; the iconography of *Life* magazine's covers has always been anything but disinterested, but perhaps never more so than in 1969. The first issue of the year featured the stunning photograph of the earth taken by *Apollo 8* showing the planet as a fragile blue sphere shining out of the black void of space. To this day it is arguably the most commonly shared image of the Space Age held in the collective consciousness of the world. Everything about the photograph and the accompanying story of the first lunar orbit is benign, triumphant, and cosmologically harmonious—the fulfillment of President Kennedy's rhetoric: "This [space] is a new ocean and I believe the United States must sail upon it."[1]

The following week's cover canceled the blue promise of this Kennedy dream with an image of Sirhan B. Sirhan—the killer of another Kennedy—in his prison cell. That summer the alternating play of space and Kennedy travail was repeated with a July 25 cover of Neil Armstrong walking to the launching pad, an August 1 shot of Ted Kennedy sitting on his porch at Hyannisport after the accident at Chappaquidick, and then an August 8 cover of the American flag planted on the moon.

The covers of all forty-nine issues of *Life* in 1969 embody the triumphs, tragedies, and banalities of America at its most schizophrenic. The year ended much as it began with cover shots of Charles Manson one week and an *Apollo 12* astronaut on the moon the next—as if the dialectic of time was that America's technological triumphs were tempered by its capability for, and culpability with, violence. A quick count of stories in *Life* reveals a nearly equal balance between two of the biggest national concerns of that time—twenty-eight on space and thirty on Vietnam. Interspersed with them are the incidents of social unrest, domestic violence, and political (mis)fortune. My Lai, Tranquility Base, Chappaquidick, Woodstock—1969 lent itself to cultural mapping by place name, even if the events were all perceived as discrete, delineated, and separate regions on the larger landscape of history as contextualized by *Life*.

Because it formed one side of the media triangle for most Americans living through the turbulent times of the Space Age and (if the collection and sale of individual issues at flea markets is any indicator) a more permanent record than either the television or newspaper sides, *Life's* rhetorical power has to be acknowledged. The narratives presented became, by and large, the received public versions because they appeared within a week of what most people were witnessing on the television screen. They authorized with text and stills the shifting image and discourse of real-time events. This was particularly true of the Manned Space Program. In the early years the magazine had exclusive contracts with the astronauts and their wives which guaranteed that they would be presented in what Tom Wolfe calls the "Presbyterian vision" of Henry Booth Luce.[2] Throughout the pivotal decade of the 1960s, the linkage of *Life* to the space program was so complete that it functioned like an aristocratic patron of an earlier century, commissioning occasional poetry from James Dickey, meditative essays from Anne Morrow Lindbergh, and, for approximately $450,000, the services of Norman Mailer to write a three-installment essay on the *Apollo 11* lunar landing. Clearly, anyone wishing to write about the astronauts or the space program had to confront the rhetorical power of *Life* magazine.

The anxiety the power of *Life* could produce creates part of the essential tension of Mailer's book-length narrative, which grew out of his commissioned articles. When *Of a Fire on the Moon* appeared a year later, the same Bob Peterson photograph of Mailer appeared on the back of the dust jacket, as if to preserve a visual link to the *Life* cover, but the front cover was even more striking. Against a black background, his name, "NORMAN MAILER," and the

title, "OF A FIRE ON THE MOON," are printed in gold lettering above a
color reproduction of René Magritte's *Le Monde Invisible,* a painting
Mailer used in the text as representative of the essential dialectic
of the moon mission. Mailer saw in the painting

> a startling image of a room with an immense rock situated in
> the center of the floor. The instant of time suggested by the
> canvas was comparable to the mood of a landscape in the in-
> stant just before something awful is about to happen, or just
> after, one could not tell. . . . Something in the acrid breath of
> the city he inhabited, some avidity emitted by a passing ma-
> chine, some tar in the residue of a nightmare, some ash from
> the memory of a cremation had gone into the painting of that
> gray stone—it was if Magritte had listened to the ending of
> one world with its comfortable chairs in the parlor, and heard
> the intrusion of a new world, silent as the windowless stone
> which grew in the room, and knowing not quite what he had
> painted, had painted his warning nonetheless. Now the world
> of the future was a dead rock, and the rock was in the room.
> (133–34)

Before opening the book, the reader has begun a journey into
the bifurcated space of (what could only be referred to with a ready
sense of irony in the 1960s) the United States. The syntactic vehicle
is Norman Mailer's prose, prose that for twenty years, through an
eclectic matrix of left-conservative romanticism and residual aptitude for and appreciation of engineering, had tried to undercut the
insidious architecture of mass values constructed on the frame of
technology and authoritarian intervention into private lives. The
uneasy stability of such a dialectical tension straining equally left
and right provides a space for Mailer to explore the terrifying possibility of a one-dimensional state of things—the counterculture
world after the revolution in works such as *Armies of the Night* and
its opposite, the technocratic blandness of corporate triumph in *Of
a Fire on the Moon*.[3] By structuring syntactic oppositions equally as

necessary, Mailer imagines himself, as he imagines Magritte, poised between a world already passed ·and a new one not understood. Because he cannot, and really does not wish to, return the world to some version of pastoral romanticism, Mailer will instead attempt to reanimate scientific humanism with dread and mystery so as to make a space for whatever romantic sensibility emerges out of close contemplation of the technological sublime.

As a writer and social activist, Mailer was historically positioned to see complex implications of the space program. Despite his protestations to the contrary, he had, in a sense, been preparing to write about the space program all his life. He is reported to have filled a 250-page notebook with a story called "An Invasion from Mars" when he was nine years old and throughout adolescence to have spent hours building elaborate working models of aircraft, even publishing an article on building models while at Boys High School in Brooklyn. At age sixteen he had been accepted by MIT to study aeronautical engineering but instead chose Harvard, where he still pursued engineering as his major.[4] When he was drafted into the army during World War II, Mailer was placed in a survey and instrumentation battalion because of his math and engineering skills. His job was to provide forward reconnaissance and fire direction for artillery through use of the same principles of calculus and vector analysis essential to ballistic missiles. This knowledge of ballistics and asymmetrical parabolas appears in his first novel, *The Naked and the Dead* (1948), in a way hauntingly anticipatory of Thomas Pynchon: "It is the curve of the death missile . . . it demonstrates the form of existence, and life and death are merely different points of observation on the same trajectory. The life viewpoint is what we see and feel astride the shell, it is the present, seeing, feeling, sensing. The death viewpoint sees the shell as a whole, knows its inexorable end, the point toward which it has been destined by inevitable physical laws."[5]

Mailer has spent his entire career trying to plot a trajectory of power in an America of "corporate enterprise controlled by forces . . . apparently at odds but secretly—and unknowingly—in alliance," which he saw as finally revealing its true coordinates in the space program.[6] In the three years preceding *Of a Fire on the Moon* he had outlined the perimeter in *Why Are We in Vietnam?* (1967), *Armies of the Night* (1968), and *Miami and the Siege of Chicago* (1969). Never content to report from the sidelines, he had run for mayor of New York City and lost because, at least in part, he believed his campaign funds dried up after news stories announced that he was being paid a huge sum to write a book about the astronauts. *Of a Fire on the Moon* begins with Mailer assessing the decade:

> John F. Kennedy had made his declaration concerning the moon not six weeks before Hemingway was dead. . . . Presumably, the moon was not listening, but if in fact, she were the receiving and transmitting station of all lunacy, then she had not been ignoring the nation since. Four assassinations later; a war in Vietnam later; a burning of Black ghettos later, hippies, drugs and many student uprisings later, one Democratic Convention in Chicago seven years later; one New York school strike later; one sexual revolution later; yes, eight years of a dramatic near-catastrophic, outright spooky decade later we were ready to make the moon. It was a decade so unbalanced in relation to previous American history that Aquarius, who had begun it by stabbing his second wife in 1960, was to finish by running in the Democratic primary for Mayor of New York. (5–6)

Except for the school strike and Mailer's own exploits, the catalog of events he gives here remains, by and large, the received assessment of 1960s. The events and Mailer's narratives about them would have been so familiar to his readers in 1970 that the exercise of power by state and federal authorities which exacerbated all of these events did not need to be emphasized.

But this latest of the bizarre events of the 1960s, the *Apollo 11* lunar landing, presented a far more formidable obstacle. Mailer cannot participate directly in this historical enterprise; that is, he cannot become an astronaut or accompany the astronauts on their voyage to the moon so he is forced to write about the technological "conquest of space" as an observer outside the power nexus, as potentially just one of more than a thousand journalists walking the sterile halls of NASA's Manned Spacecraft Center, watching the spectacle on television, and editing administrative news releases.

Like so many of the buildings that he enters to cover this story, vast areas of knowledge are sealed off to him. The sophisticated hardware of the astronauts is inaccessible to him because he does not have the technical vocabulary to comprehend its complexity; the engineers are a cheerful, helpful, and redundant clan estranged and empowered by their technological code; and even the astronauts are sealed off from any normal human response to novel experience by endless simulation of that impending experience. Their voyage to the moon is, to distort Stephen Crane, "a tale intended to be before the fact," in which everything that will happen is known and scripted in advance and the only thing new that could be added to the narrative would be disaster. It is a world in which "phenomena are only possessed of menace when they do not accommodate themselves to language-controls. Or, better, to initial-controls" (32).

The men managing this incredible feat of engineering are "part of that vast convocation of Americans, probably a majority, whom one saw in New York only on television. . . . Wasps" (10). Their bland, odorless, disciplined devotion to completing the Apollo mission efficiently without ever being able to give any adequate reason for attempting it overwhelms Mailer. So his first metadiscursive move is to declare the impossibility of writing about the space program because it speaks a language too jargon-ridden, filled with acronyms, reductive, and displaced to be comprehensible or interesting to laymen. He cannot seem to get past the outer walls of this experience to learn anything of substance so he reads the structures themselves as a text.

Mailer's anxiety about the implications of NASA's technological achievements finds its focus in the way he reacts to the architecture of that enterprise. If we extend his assertion that the moon launch is this century's equivalent of cathedral building, we can see just how culturally significant, as well as spatially dependent, is his shaping metaphor. His reference to the Vehicle Assembly Building (VAB) as the "first great cathedral of the age of technology" (55) cannot refer merely to its grand scale. All of what made cathedral building in the Middle Ages parallactic—a devotion to some unseen power in the universe taken on faith, a distorted concentration of scarce resources on one massive monument, and the spectacle of this structure rising out of a feudal landscape badly in need of some charitable Christian redistribution of wealth—make it an apt metaphor for a modern country bankrupting its social programs for the poor to support a war in Southeast Asia and an assault on the moon.

Two structures in particular figure into any close reading of *Of a Fire on the Moon,* perhaps because they represent the worst and the best that is possible for the future promised by rational science. If the future is what the Manned Spacecraft Center in Houston might make it, a closed system locked into the banal reductiveness of binomial computer absolutes, then evil rationality has won the day. If, however, the cognitively unmappable architecture of the Vehicle Assembly Building at Cape Canaveral is some reflection of the possible chaos inherent in even the most meticulously rational undertaking, then the future is still open.

This concern with the spatial, with the aesthetic future of living space, is crucial because Mailer is writing the dialectic between the possibility for totalitarianism in the organized space of NASA and the random unpredictability of the void NASA wants to explore, "outer space." His first impression of the Manned Spacecraft Center is that of carceral architecture, and his syntax reinforces that sense of constrained, flat, fixed structure:

> MSC (the Manned Spacecraft Center) was located on a tract of many acres, flat and dry as a parking lot, and at the moment of entering the gate past the guard, there was no way to determine whether one was approaching an industrial complex in which computers and electronic equipment were fashioned, or traveling into a marvelously up-to-date minimum-security prison, not a clue to whether one was visiting the largest insurance and financing corporation which had ever decided to relocate itself in the flatlands behind a fence, or if this geometrically ordered arrangement of white modern buildings, severe, ascetic, without ornament, nearly all of two or three stories but for an Administration Building of eight stories, was indeed the newest and finest kind of hospital for radiologic research. But, perhaps it was a college campus, one of those miserable brand-new college campuses with buildings white as toothpaste, windows set in aluminum casements, paths drawn by right angle or in carefully calculated zigzag to break the right angle, and a general air of studies in business administration, a college campus in short to replace the one which burned in the last revolution of the students. (8–9)

This is 1969, and in that apocalyptic summer we are to understand that a gate and guard no longer offer any distinction between high-tech manufacturing, a prison, a corporate headquarters, a hospital, or an educational institution. Nor does the architecture reveal any clue—"windowless buildings and laboratories that seemed to house computers, and did!" (9). In even the more benign comparisons, hospitals and colleges are revealed in the pejorative— a "hospital for radiologic research," not concerned so much with healing individual patients as with dissolving their suffering into the mass collation of research data, and colleges in collusion with corporate interests, devoid of the liberal arts, producing another generation of middle managers, workers, and consumers. This is still the social architecture of hierarchical power, of communication possible only in vertical direction.

The MSC is to Mailer the "brain" of NASA, and it is, in its structure, Bauhaus, utilitarian, and high modernist, even though its physical architecture is low and horizontal, moving out across a "flat anonymous and near to tree-impoverished plain" (8) between Houston and Galveston. In short, they are anonymous structures housing anonymous workers who "all seemed to wear dark pants, short-sleeve button-down white shirts and somber narrow ties . . . [with] identification badges pinned to their shirts . . . [worn] with pride" (11). They "encapsulated themselves into technological clans" based on the coded jargon of their specialties ("Yes, real Americans always spoke in code" [12]), creating a grid of knowledge and, consequently, power that according to Mailer is the basis for the name of this opening chapter, "A Loss of Ego."

The decade has wearied Mailer; he is much like Henry Adams meditating on the death of John Hay near the conclusion of *Education,* wherein he assesses the mortal wound inflicted on the nineteenth century by the Civil War and assassinations of Lincoln and Garfield.[7] The violent 1960s seem to Mailer to mark the passing of the twentieth century, though it will linger another thirty years. In a sense both are correct in their placement of the end of eras. At the time Adams was writing, rapid technological change had altered the world dramatically; electric and combustion motors were displacing steam, and the antebellum world seemed distant history. Modernism was displacing realism. For Mailer, the twentieth century conformed to the asymmetrical parabola General Edward Cummings described in *The Naked and the Dead;* the 1960s were, to him, that moment when social friction and gravity had overcome the velocity of the century and precipitated its downward acceleration.

Modernism was giving way to something he could not yet name, though he sensed its relation to the displacement of power systems signaled by electronics and the computer. If "mathematics has become the only necessary language of thought" in Adams's world of 1900, it had become even more the case for Mailer, to the extent that the adjective "necessary" was now superfluous.[8] He begins *Of a Fire on the Moon* fearing that those who believe that the key to unlocking the universe is measure, rather than metaphor, are winning the ideological struggle. At least this is what the first glimpse of NASA's structure in the architecture of the MSC and what his contact with the engineers and astronauts signal to him.

Mailer's view of the Vehicle Assembly Building at Cape Canaveral is more visceral. Referring to it as the "body" of NASA, his meditation on it is a revealing piece of prose, and I quote it here at length because, besides being a catalog of existing architectural structures of political significance which are capable of being subsumed by this huge new infrastructure, it is also a syntactic simulacrum of an ambivalent exploration of technical expertise. His prose expands, shifts, and becomes vertiginous in its attempt to encompass the enormous complexity of the structure:

> The Vehicle Assembly Building, 526 feet high, a building just about as large as the combined volume of the Merchandise Mart in Chicago and the Pentagon. . . . The doors to the four bays were each over forty stories and therefore high enough and wide enough to take in through their portals the UN Building or the Statue of Liberty. Yet for all its size, the VAB was without decorations inside, rather a veritable shipyard and rigging of steel girders which supported whole floors capable of being elevated and lowered then rolled in and out like steel file drawers in order to encircle each rocket with adjustable working platforms from either side. Since some of these platforms had three complete stories contained within them, the interior of the VAB was a complexity of buildings within buildings which had been first maneuvered then suspended ten and twenty and thirty stories above the ground. Because the sides were usually open, one could look out from

the platforms to other constellations of girders and buildings and could look down from whichever great height to the floor of the VAB, sometimes as much as forty stories below. Note however: one was still inside a closed space, and the light which filtered through translucent panels rising from floor to ceiling was dim, hardly brighter than the light in a church or an old railroad terminal. One lost in consequence any familiar sense of recognition—you could have been up in the rigging of a bridge built beneath the dome of some partially constructed and enormous subterranean city, or you could have been standing on the scaffolding of an unfinished but monumental cathedral, beautiful in this dim light, this smoky concatenation of structure upon structure, of breadths and vertigos and volumes of open space beneath the ceiling, tantalizing views of immense rockets hidden by their clusters of work platforms. One did not always know whether one was on a floor, a platform, a bridge, a fixed or impermanent part of this huge shifting ironwork of girders and suspended walkways. (52–54)

Mailer's selection of structures that will fit inside the VAB is anything but disinterested choice. The Statue of Liberty, an engineering marvel of the previous century and always a symbol of the promise to immigrants, suggests America's visionary compact even in this new enterprise. The United Nations, functioning as it does as the latest geopolitical hope for peace and stability, can also be subsumed by this structure, as can the Pentagon, the current geopolitical center of power, and the Chicago Merchandise Mart, a monument to consumer capitalism.

The linkage of the VAB to cathedrals and grand train stations is an impulse toward architectural pastiche in the eye of the beholder, if not the architect. But again, beyond the immensity of enclosed space captured by a cathedral like the one at Chartres or of a railway station like Union or Grand Central are the cultural narratives of feudalism and industrialism. Mailer is not the first to see a historical analogy between the impact of the railroad and the space program on the American landscape, but his use of it is focused not on how each influenced the imagination or the economy but on how it visually altered that landscape.[9]

If the VAB is comprehensible only by way of metaphor with some earlier testimony to mankind's collective impulse, the work performed within its enclosure has no parallel. As a new technology, the VAB and all the specialized engineering, acronyms, and division of authority conform to a new distribution of power and knowledge and as such might lend themselves to an exploration of the 1960s and 1970s in light of what Alvin Toffler referred to that same year as the rise of a new and more fluid "ad hocracy" continually realigning itself project by project instead of bureaucratically layering itself into vertical rigidity.[10]

Mailer's deep concern is with the *cost* of the manned space program, Project Apollo in particular, on the psyche of a nation, if not a world. The cheerful, redundant quality of all the engineers he meets in Houston disturbs Mailer, not so much because they are such positivists but because they seem to place so much faith in the power of technique and rational system. Because everything related to the manned launches is so precisely and minutely worked out in detail and computer simulated ad infinitum, any sense of romance, mystery, or intrigue, any space for *individuality* in the outcome, has been minimized to the lowest common denominator. These technicians and engineers are the most visible examples of NASA's total embrace of Taylorism and a positive economy of time that has mapped every second of the lunar mission to "extract from time ever more available moments and, from each moment ever more useful forces."[11]

Mailer objects to what NASA has created in its meticulously developed flight plan for the astronauts: a moment-by-moment narrative of the journey to the moon and back that leaves not one second unaccounted for and no possibility for surprise. This is the very heart of the vast contradictions and accelerating opposites that tormented Mailer into attempting this book. As he has been educated by the experience of total access to overwhelming amounts of technical information, Mailer has found himself standing at the base of a techno-scientific structure grown so enormous in the last twenty-five years that even language seems about to fail.

It is this dialectic of bureaucratic rationality driven to display its prowess in an essentially irrational act of sending men to the moon just to prove it can be done that allows Mailer enough space to create in the persona of "Aquarius" a residual romantic who can interrogate this project. In a sense this is Mailer's way of coping with a problem he had not had to face in any of his previous writing projects—the absolute separation of observer and event.

Whereas *Armies of the Night* is a record of Mailer's personal participation in the march on Washington, *Of a Fire on the Moon* has to be a narrative in which Mailer is sitting in the viewing stand and not atop the rocket. There is no way he can participate except as an observer among thousands of other journalist-observers, so if he is to produce anything more compelling than just another vivid description of the awesome power of the launch he must enter into the event from an oblique angle. Aquarius offers him that entry because his romantic sensibility will resuscitate all the moribund mythology and mystery present in the project names and objectives of NASA. Starting with the moon itself, this narrative voice will explore the irrational avenues of dread and dreams to maintain some sense of the moon as a force of lunacy and a repository of the poetic.

This is after all the project Mailer has set for himself—to reclaim from the languages of science, bureaucracy and media hype a sense of something ragged, raw, unpredictable, inefficient, and above all human. The key issue is whether he can develop a discourse that captures the enormity and complexity of this rationalist project and at the same time subverts the essential positivism that enables it to displace a more irrational cosmology. So the narrative he finally writes from the point of view of Aquarius is a narrative of accretion, one that texturally as well as textually reinforces the sheer volume of minute detail necessary to carry off a project like the moon landing, a narrative that holds to his belief that "if the universe is a lock, its key is metaphor, not measure," by continually extending the measure of those metaphors until the images and disparate ideas they link are as complex and interconnected in scale as the VAB itself.

Mailer must, as Laurence Goldstein puts it, "negotiate through at least three languages in which no literary masterpiece had ever been composed: the scientific, the bureaucratic . . . and the language of hype." [12] The subject of *Of a Fire on the Moon* is, as Chris Anderson has observed, Mailer's effort to write a compelling narrative of the moon shot, not the moon shot itself. [13] As the book grew from the three articles he wrote for *Life,* Mailer structured it in such a way that it took the same sort of overlap and redundancy inherent in a project like Apollo. The three sections—"Aquarius," "Apollo," and "The Age of Aquarius"—are all, in a sense, progressive versions of the same story, any one of which would carry the reader to the moon and back, but the other two versions are there in case of a rhetorical failure of the first.

The first section, "Aquarius," focuses self-reflexively on the way bureaucratic language subsumes the individual in its syntactic penchant for nominalization and the passive voice. It is Aquarius/Mailer's personal account of his writing the piece. The chapters within it, "A Loss of Ego," "The Psychology of Astronauts," "Some Origins of the Fire," "The Greatest Week," and "A Dream of the Future's Face," seek to discover the dispersed and disorienting organizational structure of NASA. The locus of "A Loss of Ego" is the Manned Spacecraft Center outside of Houston, Texas, where, as we have seen, the carceral architecture and cheerful discipline of the redundant engineers decentered Mailer's persona. "The Psychology of Astronauts" examines the last vestige of individuality left in the program, the astronauts-elect, and finds them as flat and inaccessible as the binomial code of the computers that sit behind glass partitions: "Aldrin spoke of . . . 'various contingencies that can develop,' of 'a wider variety of trajectory conditions'—he was talking about not being able to join up, wandering through space, lost forever to life in that short eternity before they expired of hunger and thirst. Small hint of that in these verbal formulations. . . . The heart of astronaut talk, like the heart of all bureaucratic talk, was a jargon which could easily be converted to computer programming" (25).

The chapter also examines the paucity of response available to the press assigned to cover a story so momentous but so packaged and bland that the media become just another bureaucratic extension of the project. "Some Origins of the Fire" shifts the location of NASA's power to the Kennedy Space Center in Florida and sets up the interesting contrast between the organizational structure in Houston that appears to be the triumph of corporate verticality and division of labor and a more protean arrangement that is emerging and as yet not fully understood but is best reflected in the design of the VAB. "Some Origins of the Fire" is very possibly the most lyrical chapter of the entire book. Mailer begins with a meditation on the "prairie sadness" of the abandoned launch complexes at Cape Canaveral, then shifts the scene to the fanciful contrast between Wernher Von Braun speaking imperially at a country club VIP reception, while an imaginary mill worker sleeps in his car, waiting out the long night before the launch by the causeway. He concludes the chapter with a truly sublime description of the launch itself:

Two mighty torches of flame like the wings of a yellow bird of fire flew over a field, covered a field with brilliant yellow bloomings of flame, and in the midst of it, white as a ghost, white as the white of Melville's Moby Dick, white as the shrine of the Madonna in half the churches of the world, this slim angelic mysterious ship of stages rose without sound out of its incarnation of flame and began to ascend slowly into the sky, slow as Melville's Leviathan might swim, slowly as we might swim upward in a dream looking for the air. (100)

This chapter is offered as antidote to the linguistic ills of corporate science. Perhaps because it takes place in a place still raw and fecund, the estuarial swamp of Florida, there is in Aquarius's mind still hope for some coexistence between the slovenly natural world and the efficient sterility of NASA's dream of the future. By contrast, the ironically titled "The Greatest Week" returns the reader not only to Houston but to an account of the lunar landing stifled by hype and thorough bureaucratic planning. This is the chapter in which Mailer more or less sets up the reader with an account that fulfills the reader's sense of what television had already produced, even to the point of inserting italicized communication transcript to serve as a form of intertextual soundtrack to accompany his mediated description of what television is depicting. As such it becomes third-generation narrative. It is a chapter about the difficulty of doing anything more with the story, and it serves as a contrast to what Mailer pulls off in his central section, where he takes the reader through the launch again, but this time in a way that makes the technological immensity of the project truly sublime. Before he can do that, however, Aquarius must map one more site of power in "A Dream of the Future's Face."

The occasion for this chapter is an invitation to a party at an ascetically modern home in Houston. The hosts are wealthy Europeans of taste and refinement who have in their foyer the Magritte that has given Aquarius his central metaphor of the technological future as a "dead rock in a room." Also present at the party in a way not unlike the art objects displayed throughout the home is a black Ivy League professor whose adversarial dialogue with Aquarius delineates further the social concerns of the time. Earlier Aquarius had lumped the black population in the disfranchised heap of America's poor who were expected to benefit at some later date from the scientific advances trickling over the sides of NASA's $20 billion pie, but now he is confronted by an articulate individual who views Aquarius as being far more closely aligned with the "WASPs" who have taken the moon than with the racial and ethnic cultures that will now be even further separated from actual and ideological power.

Coming as it does near the end of Mailer's initial mapping of the complex topography of NASA's organizational structure, "A Dream of the Future's Face" serves as a recapitulation of the conflict between rational systems and romanticism that initially leaves Aquarius depressed and disoriented. The troubling juxtaposition of rock and room in the Magritte, the somewhat racist contention that a black cosmology privileges magic and dream, and the professor's assertion that "technology begins when men are ready to believe that the sins of the fathers are not visited on the sons," and are thereby empowered to challenge the gods, leads finally to Aquarius's understanding that the "Twentieth Century was a century which looked to explain the psychology of the dream and instead entered the topography of the dream. The real had become more fantastic than the imagined" (141).

Forced to choose between seeing the moon shot as a divine or satanic mission or as a "species of sublimation for the profoundly unmanageable violence of man" (152), Aquarius chooses the Manichaean option. He has come to accept that the "verbal banality of reaction" to events that "might yet dislocate eternity" was not merely "an indication of the disease of our time, so advanced in one lobe, so underdeveloped in another," but instead some evidence of deitistic desperation: "—there might not be time to develop men to speak like Shakespeare as they departed on heavenly ships" (150).

Having thus shifted his ideological stance however slightly, Mailer has pulled off an interesting rhetorical move. In the first 152 pages he has functioned as the iconoclast, bringing down the image of NASA as triumphant testimony to engineering efficiency and returning the astronauts to operators of dangerously complex machines, finding in the process some glimmer of the grand and heroic pulsing through the circuits. He has put the reader in a position to accept the impossibility of breathing eloquence into technology, to settle, as it were, for a spectacle best left to the passive transmission of television. The next 276 pages belie that premise.

The vast middle section of *Of a Fire on the Moon*, "Apollo," no longer focuses on the difficulty of reporting the moon shot but instead provides a detailed chronological account of the mission. Mailer is showing that, indeed, he can master the technical codes and capture the power of NASA's technological achievement, but while he is doing this he is also deconstructing the rational premise of science and showing it to be a "technology [that] is not quits with magic" (161). By calling forth all the anomalies, indeterminacies, and speculative theories that haunt the finally uncertain halls of science, he is able to weaken its power to displace the poetic discourse of the moon as repository of love and lunacy with a moon remapped as a dead gray rock. *Weaken* is the operative word here because, in the process of assimilating the jargon and codes necessary to write this middle section of *Of a Fire on the Moon*, Mailer also records the erosion of his resistance to the engineering feat he is reporting. In keeping with the Manichaeanism of the entire narrative, he makes physics and engineering into religious metaphors: "Physics is the church, and engineering the most devout sinner. Physics is the domain of beauty, law, order, awe, and mystery of the purest sort; engineering is partial observance of the laws, and puttering with machines that never work quite as they should work: engineering, like acts of sin, is the process of proceeding boldly into complex and often forbidding matters about which one does not know enough" (230).

Having linked sin and engineering with bold exploration, rather than with error, Aquarius has made a space for technological advance inside his own cosmology. Taking risks, taking action without any certainty of the outcome, discovering the way along the way—this is what Mailer has spent his lifetime advocating.

Of a Fire on the Moon is itself an example of textual engineering, he would have us believe, therefore engineering can be accommodated, appropriated, co-opted, and its technical triumph in the form of a lunar landing celebrated not for its pure precision but for its incredible faith. The background material Mailer borrows from *First on the Moon* and the NASA transcripts reveals how any of the so-called minor systems failures could have resulted in disaster.

These first two sections, "Aquarius" and "Apollo," would seem to exhaust the possibilities for writing about the moon shot, and as technical achievement they do. But the implications of what has been wrought by this historic event have not yet been examined, and this is the subject of "The Age of Aquarius," the final section. What began in hostility and distrust toward a WASP culture that denuded everything of naturalness and then grudgingly appropriated the achievements of those WASPs by making them less totalized in their scientific certainty must now, finally, confront the consequences not only of the achievement but also the shift in perspective it has brought about.

The short final section, "The Age of Aquarius," takes place on Cape Cod, in Provincetown, among the counterculture friends who reside at this site where the Puritan presence first made itself known in America. The weeks Aquarius has spent in Texas and Florida among the confining and disorienting structures of a technological future have changed him enough that he can no longer embrace the hedonism that passes for degraded romanticism. He wants to rail out at "the army he was in, treacherous, silly, overconfident and vain, haters and despisers of everything tyrannical, phony, plastic and overbearing in American life [who] had dropped out" while the WASPs have with great discipline "taken the moon" (440).

The events of the summer have strained Aquarius's faith in the people he has always championed—the marginalized voices of the creative, the violent, the violently creative, the creatively violent, and, generally, the dissipated detritus of the greatest of all capitalist societies. Even the "weak magic" of burying a junk automobile that has been cut and welded into a crude sculpture not unlike the lunar module cannot, in its ritual disposal of technology, restore him. At its nadir, the poetic seems imperiled by technocratic self-validating epistemology on one side and by aesthetic trivialization on the other. But Aquarius will not allow his narrative to end with the apocalyptic summer of 1969. He returns to the metadiscourse of how hard it is to write anything substantive about the moon shot and, searching for some angle that will aestheticize the project and hold open the possibility of a world not so closed, Aquarius goes to look at one of the hermetically sealed moon rocks on display in Houston. This is not the dominating rock in the room of the Magritte painting, a rock that spoke of a future without windows. This is a tiny, weathered cinder nearly lost in the room housing it. Weary of all that has been lost that summer, Aquarius stands before the tiny rock as a man whose will to resist has been broken. In this state of full romantic sentimentality,

> he stood in quiet before that object from the moon, that rock which gave him certitude enough to know he would write his book and in some part applaud the feat and honor the astro-nauts because the expedition to the moon was finally a venture which might help to disclose the nature of the Lord and the Lucifer who warred for us. . . . he had come to believe . . . that probably we had to explore into outer space, for technology had penetrated the modern mind to such a depth that voy-ages in space might have become the last way to discover the metaphysical pits of that world of technique which choked the pores of modern consciousness—yes, we might have to go out into space until the mystery of new discovery would force us to regard the world once again as poets. (471)

And so, like the magnificent but disorienting interior of the Ve-hicle Assembly Building, the new age that is being born is one that shifts, offers no vantage point from which to view the whole, but in its sublimity may yet save itself because Aquarius believes it will require a poetics unavailable to computers.

In the final analysis, Mailer is still tethered to an approach to the space program and to aesthetics that grounds itself in modernism's celebration of the individual. Like Updike, Bellow, and Wolfe, his project is parabolic, returning the implications of man's exploration of space to earthly inquiries into his own response. Unlike the previous authors, though, Mailer sees in the emerging technocratic state that has made this moon landing possible a future not of despair but of anesthesia: "He was adrift. If he tried to conceive of a like perspective in the decade before him, he saw not one structure to society but two: if the social world did not break down into revolutions and counterrevolutions, into police and military rules of order with sabotage, guerrilla war and enclaves of resistance, if none of this occurred, then there would certainly be a society of reason, but its reason would be the logic of the computer" (141).

And, of course, dwelling within this society would be an "irrational society . . . [where] the art of the absurd would reign in defiance against the computer" (142). But by the end of *Of a Fire on the Moon*, Mailer no longer seems to hold much stock in that alternative. He has applauded technique and left the field. It will be the task of Thomas Pynchon and Don DeLillo to explore fully the zone of irrationality that dwells in the land of science.

The beauty of the Dune's Casino de Paris show

is that it will be beyond art, beyond

dance, beyond spectacle. . . .

[It will be] a behemoth

piece of American

calculus, like Project

Mercury. —Tom Wolfe,

The Kandy-Kolored Tangerine-

Flake Streamline Baby

5 Desert Space and the High Frontier:
Tom Wolfe as Text Pilot

In the novels of Bellow and Updike the presence and the status of the media and their relation to the lives of the main characters were important to the work of Sammler and Angstrom. Both authors foregrounded the selective distortion of events as they were observed firsthand and then narrated in the press. Clearly, something of the modern world's ability to denude experience into the experience of *having experience represented* troubled these novelists of social realism. The clean line between individual lives of quotidian concreteness and the vicarious world of fictional sensation has been erased by an informationally complex, globally linked mediated world. Sammler cannot get beyond the "Vista-Vision" spectacle of modern warfare. Harry Angstrom is the obliging double-blind typesetter of some unknown reporter's account of events which he knows occurred very differently because they happened to him. Try as they might to imagine it otherwise, the things that happen in the world seem to happen for them in the linear space of newsprint, just as their lives play out along the linearity of the text.

As readers of *Mr. Sammler's Planet* and *Rabbit Redux*, we are even further removed from the experience of the world in the sense that we are reading about a character reading about the world we imagine we inhabit. The same images and events common to the reader's daily media experience are now recontextualized as literary memory as well. Popular culture and world affairs—the civil and racial strife of the cities, military conflicts in Vietnam, Israel, and Greece, television and movies like *2001: A Space Odyssey,* and, in particular, the space triumphs by Russians and Americans—everything is doubly linear, doubly removed from immediate apprehension. The world of events has been aestheticized into a literary setting important only in its effect on the individual psyche trying to impose some order in a private world. Edited for time and space, the received narratives of recent world events become, even in fiction, neat tiles in an emerging mosaic of national interest still dependent on its Puritan and Western motifs.

Even Norman Mailer's thoughts on how many of "the most important events in America seemed to take place in all of the lonely spaces—as if the Twentieth Century had become the domain of all the great and empty territories" maintains the tone.[1] Certainly, Tom Wolfe's exploration of the early years of the space program in *The Right Stuff* buys into a genealogical history that comes right out of the western movie. But then again, so did some of the astronauts themselves.

In his memoir, *Carrying the Fire,* astronaut Michael Collins describes the decorative patch worn by test pilots at Edwards Air Force Base as "a futuristic, aerodynamic shape escaping from a sandy, cactus-bedecked background into a blue-black sky" and beneath this scene, a Latin inscription, "Ad Inexplorata." As iconographic shorthand of how closely linked are the images of the old frontier and its successor, the high frontier of space, the patch is marvelous. Other than the majestic topography of Monument Valley there are few visual objects so immediately evocative of popular conceptions of the West as the stunted desert vegetation of cactus and Joshua tree—those grotesque caricatures of men with arms outstretched to the emptiness around them. What better visual text could there be to show the present as a Newtonian moment of time and velocity frozen between the desert of the past and the vast dark desert of the future? Collins goes on to reinforce the linkage of old West and new space by evoking the gender stereotypes of popular westerns:

> It was also dry and hot and windy and isolated, and not at all what a proper Bostonian—my wife—would expect as a nursery for her firstborn. I knew this, and winced, but I also knew that she would prevail, and neither Joshua tree nor rattlesnake nor sandstorm would dim her New England resolve, nor her ability to change it! After all, in a historic sense, it was a place for upstarts. . . . I also knew that despite the desolation, the one-hundred-plus heat, the perpetual howling of the wind, this was the place.[2]

The history of the Manned Space Program has, from its inception, consciously or unconsciously borrowed the actual and mental landscape of the American wilderness for its new excursion. Experimental aviation and rocketry needed vast open spaces well away from urban centers. In the early years of flight testing before World War II, it had been the desolate coastal sites along the eastern seaboard, places like Kitty Hawk on the Outer Banks of North Carolina, Langley Field in Virginia, and the Patuxent River in Maryland that provided a similar environment, but only to the east over the ocean. These sites were bordered by populous areas inland, which limited testing in that direction because of the danger posed by overflights. That same proximity to urban centers helped maintain a certain discipline and decorum within the operation. Aviators were officers and officers were gentlemen and all that.

After the war, when the new branch of the service, the air force, broke away from the army, it looked west to Colorado and the high deserts of New Mexico, Nevada, and California for flight testing precisely because the resistance of those places to habitation afforded the space and the secrecy needed to test jet- and rocket-powered supersonic aircraft. Because of their remoteness from the more civilized centers of power, these test sites took on the character of frontier towns. Physically, the buildings were makeshift, temporary, ramshackle, or all of the above. Conditions were primitive; the challenges of these duty stations attracted people who were predominantly young, almost exclusively male, held egocentrism to be a virtue, and understood high mortality statistics. The same virtues of self-reliance, laconic speech, dry humor, and resistance to regulation that have always been part of the western stereotype began to emerge at places like Edwards Air Force Base. Tom Wolfe describes Muroc Field in the late 1940s (before it became Edwards): "Muroc [Field] was up in the high elevations of the Mojave Desert. It looked like some fossil landscape that had long since been left behind by the rest of terrestrial evolution. It was full of huge dry lake beds, the biggest being Rogers Lake. Other than sagebrush the only vegetation was Joshua trees, twisted freaks of the plant world that . . . stood out in silhouette on the fossil wasteland like some arthritic nightmare."[3]

The inhabitants of this desert space, the engineers and test pilots, are cast by Wolfe into the roles of those hearty men who first pioneered and learned to live in the harsh climate of remote existence. They are a brotherhood, bound by solitude and shared mission. Anyone untested by the rigors of that experience is suspect: "When the screen door banged and a man walked through the door into the saloon, every eye in the place checked him out. If he wasn't known as somebody who had something to do with flying at Muroc, he would be eyed like some lame goddamned mouseshit sheepherder from Shane" (52).

These passages taken together provide an interesting catalog of western symbols. Michael Collins's reference to his wife's probable reaction to the Mojave Desert base is as neat a culturally engendered scenario as *High Noon* or *Angel and the Bad Man*: the eastern wife, pregnant, accompanies her adventuresome husband west, prepared to unleash all her New England domestic skill to tame a territory hostile to her. Wolfe's description of Edwards Air Force Base typifies those narratives of place that map the western landscape as harsh, inhospitable—antagonistic nature. The saloon scene reference to *Shane* is richer still in its intertextual allusion to a West already transforming itself from open range to delineated space and the hostility to that change displayed by the old fraternity.

In all the passages there is that element of wistfulness for the sublime that has been driven out by a ceaselessly encroaching technical civilization. As Bellow, Updike, and to a degree Mailer have made clear, the present condition of the culture, reflected in the behavior and architecture of its cities, seems to be one of moral and physical collapse. The technical support services needed to handle the burgeoning masses are outdated and insufficient. Cultural anthropologist Edward T. Hall is studying urban centers such as New York as "behavioral sinks" and finding that overcrowding in humans produces the same aberrancy and disease present in animal populations that have reproduced beyond their innate territorial needs.[4] Even though food and shelter might be adequate, the innate requirements of space have been compromised. So the West, as a place of space (if not grace), loomed large in the collective psyche of midcentury America.

In the 1960s and early 1970s, television and film were saturated with westerns celebrating the individual and the unbordered. The myth of the West had always been about limitless space even though the reality of the West has always been the mediation of that space by the technology accompanying the explorers of it. The frontier enabled the dreamers and the misfits in the nineteenth century temporarily to displace themselves from the strictures of town, church, and culturally imposed notions of domesticity and yet to carry into those desert spaces enough firepower to seize the technological high ground over indigenous man and beast (if any distinction was made). That same frontier provided the staging area in the second half of the twentieth century for journeys into other unmapped regions. What the Colt revolver and the Hawken and Winchester rifles were to the trappers and plainsmen, the rockets at Alamogordo and experimental jets at Muroc Field were to the mavericks of the military: the technical devices that enabled them to extend the frontier at the expense of colonizing and delimiting it.

Just one example of this ongoing appropriation of the West is Sidney Pollack's 1972 film *Jeremiah Johnson,* a movie that gives new meaning to the stock disclaimer "based on a novel by" (in this case Vardis Fisher's *Mountain Man*). It opens with a scene of a young man, apparently just released from military service in the Mexican War of 1847, disembarking from a flatboat somewhere along the Missouri River. He still wears the vestiges of his uniform and carries with him the sidearm of the times, a .36-caliber cap-and-ball revolver. Little is revealed about him, but we infer that the war has changed him so much that to go back to the quotidian world of the East is no longer an option. He is instead heading for the high frontier of the Rockies to make his living as a trapper—a solitary, precarious life filled with a thousand ways to screw up and die. His only edge is the technology he brings with him, flint and steel, case-hardened knives, firearms, leghold traps, and the like. He will use that technology and these open spaces for profit, selling his fur pelts for the food and manufactured supplies, powder, shot, and traps that allow him to live at a distance from the spurned civilization whose economic structure he helps sustain.

The illusion of that separation from the East is shattered by army scouts, vindictive Indians, ignorant settlers, and an exploitive economy. The plot turns dark and existential after Johnson reluctantly aids the U.S. Cavalry's efforts to rescue a snowbound expedition. En route they trespass on Indian tribal burial grounds. In retaliation, Indians kill Johnson's squaw and burn his home. Johnson hunts down and kills the Indians responsible. But now he is known as "Crow Killer," and the desert spaces have become just another literal and figurative place to do cutthroat business. All that is left him at the end is the Canadian Northwest, some new desert of the mind.

Jeremiah Johnson as a Lukácian "prehistory of the present"—a

parable of the fierce ambivalence of Vietnam, of cultural transgres-
sions and violent consequences, of the displacement of a country of
the mind by the infinitely more complex country of experience—
has fused for me in some curious melted crosswire of memory
with Wolfe's precursor to *The Right Stuff*, published in *Rolling Stone*
about that same time.

Just as Mailer's *Of a Fire on the Moon* began as a series of magazine articles, so did *The Right Stuff*. In 1973 Wolfe published in
Rolling Stone a four-part series titled "Post-Orbital Remorse." Each
installment had a separate subheading: "The Brotherhood of the
Right Stuff," "How the Astronauts Fell from Cowboy Heaven," "The
Dark Night of the Ego," and "The Last Great Galactic Flash." What
links the film *Jeremiah Johnson* and the pieces that became *The
Right Stuff* is their shared attitude toward the myth of the West;
both appropriate its landscape to explore the historical moment
of the 1970s. What Wolfe saw in the unique rhetorical force of
America's space program in its early stages—the X-series rocket
plane tests and Project Mercury—was precisely its appeal as "a
cowboy operation": "We were riding hell for leather to try to catch
up with the Russians. To find out if there were Indians over the
next hill, what you did was ride at full gallop over the next hill.
That way you were *sure* to find out: there was no time to be fooling
around with scouting reports. . . . It was cowboy stuff, Tom, and it
was a beautiful time."[5]

Wolfe locates much of what has changed in the American
landscape in the peculiar nature of Project Mercury, which was
initially presented to the public as a rational research project, but
then, somehow, changed from a traditional scientist-engineer–test
subject paradigm into a public spectacle that served the national
interest at a critical juncture. That critical moment in *The Right
Stuff* is the disjuncture between the public perception of the astronaut program's progress and the actuality of its problems. Wolfe's
thesis is that Project Mercury had so much media buildup that

it was impossible to cancel the program even though it was far riskier and far behind the more established (and, to Wolfe, more appealing) X-series aerodynamic approach.

Since the 1986 *Challenger* tragedy, the public has learned just what risks NASA has always taken to maintain its image, but this was hardly the case in the early years. At that time, when the Cold War was at its most intense, print and broadcast journalism touted the technical achievements of NASA with little criticism beyond noting the disproportionate expense of its projects. And even though Wolfe treats the early history of the space program more iconoclastically than do most other narratives of the Space Age, he never really questions its necessity, just its methods and location. The ground on which *The Right Stuff* is built is familiar. The labor of Puritanism, the myth of the West, the technological emergence of mass society and spectacle, the status of history, and issues of gender, race, and class are all sites of conflict.

The Right Stuff examines the early history of manned space-flight for rhetorical clues that might shed some light on how a project that initially operated in such relative media obscurity became the full-blown spectacle that is so familiar to all the readers of *Mr. Sammler's Planet, Rabbit Redux,* and *Of a Fire on the Moon.* For Wolfe, the synchronic moment that forms the narrative core of the Space Age is not 1969 but instead a durative span ranging from the end of World War II up to the end of Project Mercury in 1963.

In this attempt to recover the human dimension of the astronauts Wolfe pushes beyond the earlier efforts of Oriani Fallaci (*If the Sun Dies*) and Norman Mailer (*Of a Fire on the Moon*) by, in a sense, reversing the polarity. Where Fallaci and Mailer found the selfless technical blandness of astronauts and engineers to be what one would expect such a project to produce, Wolfe finds a deliberate effort on the part of NASA and mainstream media to portray this image when, in fact, the astronauts were quite different. For him, the tension that pulls at the whole astronaut program is the need to take massive egos of test pilots accustomed to working actively in relative autonomy and harness them into a bureaucratic structure designed to make those roles purely symbolic and passive.

This "routinization of charisma"—a term Pynchon borrows from Max Weber—seemed worthy of comment to so many writers in the 1970s because they still held out hope for some alternative to mass man in a society of spectacle. A key linkage to Bellow's and Updike's social realist fiction and the literary journalism of Mailer and Wolfe is this shared desire to privilege the individual and the autonomous. For Bellow it is found in the interior and private leadership of the engaged intellectual whose radicalism stems from a knowledge of philosophy and history. For Updike it is also the interior space of individual lives, even the inarticulate lives of the working class. Mailer finds hope finally, not in the dismissive excesses of the current counterculture, but rather in some new millennial urgency made possible by men searching the stars for God. And for Wolfe the model is the terse, analytical test pilot trained nearly to the point of automation but at heart still the solo warrior, the coarse western hero who pushes into the unknown territory trusting his instincts, reflexes, and luck to see him through.

During the six-year gestational period of *The Right Stuff,* the geographical distance between the Mojave Desert and NASA headquarters at Langley, Virginia, began to stand as representative of the psychological and technical distance separating the two approaches to putting men into space. The *Rolling Stone* articles had situated the astronauts in the currently familiar technoscape of Houston and Cape Canaveral. Employing a colloquial second-person point of view to mimic the astronauts, Wolfe foregrounded their metadiscursive problem: an inability to articulate an experience so technically specific, yet ineffable, as spaceflight. They are men of massive ego but rational and reticent, trained for autonomous judgment, a technical elite of a new age thrust into media celebrity that runs contrary to all that has set them apart: "We also became a little self-conscious about the fact that our shirts didn't really fit, our ties didn't belong in this decade, and our suits didn't look right for standing up on a platform in front of several hundred people in. NASA didn't want us to wear our officer's dress, because they were projecting a non-military image."[6]

Because a glib facility with language is not part of their job description, Wolfe argues, they become inadvertent prey for the media image makers, who turn them into an idealized middle-class vision of the American hero. They become middle-American urban citizens, not mavericks out West, and it is the implications of that stereotype which form the thematic center of Wolfe's book.

The West as the site of individual triumph over the leveling bureaucracy of mass values is central to *The Right Stuff*. As actual geography, the location is Edwards Air Force Base in the high desert of California. It is not incidental that much of the first half of the book centers on the X-series rocket plane testing going on there after World War II. Military test pilot Chuck Yeager, who is barely mentioned in Wolfe's "Post-Orbital Remorse," becomes the most recent incarnation of the "fastest gun in the West" in *The Right Stuff*. By writing the obscure, if not suppressed, history of Yeager's pioneering exploits in breaking the sound barrier, Wolfe puts in place an entire setting borrowed from literature and film of the American West. Wolfe's version of the world of the test pilots at Edwards is hardly distinguishable from the myth of the frontier town.

What *The Right Stuff* accomplishes in the early chapters is cultural preservation of the West and its space for rugged (read "manly") individualism. The representative anecdote is Yeager's refusal to scrub his scheduled X-1 flight even though he has broken two ribs in a fall from, naturally, a horse. Using a sawed-off broom handle to give him enough leverage to seal the hatch on the X-1, Yeager goes on to break the sound barrier for the first time in history.[7] This feat places Yeager at the top of an elusive metaphorical pyramid that combines talent, instinct, and luck to reveal, at least for the moment, some sign of "the right stuff." To Wolfe, the process of proving oneself is an interior divination based on outward performance: "All the hot young fighter jocks began trying to test the limits themselves in a superstitious way. They were like believing Presbyterians of a century before who used to probe their own experience to see if they were truly among *the elect*" (30).

There is in the tone of these early chapters a nostalgia for this familiar narrative of laconic self-reliance which will be contrasted with the total manipulation of the astronauts' environment. At Langley Research Center in Virginia (named for the Samuel Langley who figures prominently in Henry Adams's *Education,* particularly "The Dynamo and the Virgin" chapter), the astronauts would be subjected to endless mechanical flight simulators designed to make the novelty of zero-gravity spaceflight a totally conditioned response.

The astronaut program situated back East threatened to have all the constrictions of the civilization those out West had put behind them. One was never alone, protocols had to be followed, permission granted, time carefully allocated. The astronauts would be passive subjects monitored by teams of scientists, not active pilots pushing the performance limits of their machines. The difference was as distinct as the difference between "capsule" and "spacecraft."

All that is passive, helpless, and sealed off is contained in the referent, *capsule,* whereas an astronaut piloting a spacecraft is active, engaged, and in control. As Wolfe demonstrates, their exposure in *Life* gave them authority, and the astronauts began to lobby for semantic changes as well as system redesigns that reflected shifts in perception. The realignment of power in the fluid dynamic of NASA infrastructure is a key issue in *The Right Stuff.* Military rank no longer locks the astronauts into a rigid hierarchical bureaucracy because their status as volunteers for a hazardous mission has given them access to the upper echelons of government and business. All it has cost them is their privacy and their individual personal histories. The role of the news media in creating a celebrity status for the astronauts and, simultaneously, policing the borders of that status is even more central to *The Right Stuff* than it has been in the other narratives discussed so far.

By writing a history of the space program that shows how the astronauts rewrote the roles spelled out for them, Wolfe can reclaim a space for American individual will. To do this in *The Right Stuff*, he interweaves the successful though never highly media-saturated narrative of the aerodynamic X-series rocket plane tests at Edwards with the troubled media darling, the ballistic missile approach of Project Mercury. In the beginning, a stable world of high-performance flight testing exists in the remote deserts of the West. Like any self-contained society, the hierarchy is in place, the rules are understood, and avenues of prestige and power are understood by all. This is the linear trajectory of manned flight from the Wright brothers to spaceflight. Suddenly, all is destabilized by Soviet advances in spaceflight and America's crash response, known as Project Mercury.

What had been a scientific/engineering enterprise designed to perfect an aerodynamic spacecraft that would be controlled by a pilot from powered ascent to powered landing became, instead, a ballistic exercise that would launch a man into space with about as much control as an artillery shell. By shifting the setting of *The Right Stuff* back and forth between the achievements at Edwards and the failures at Cape Canaveral in the late 1950s and early 1960s, Wolfe is able to document just how important the ideological value of putting a man into space was to the international prestige of the United States. Everything at Edwards is represented in positive values of Yankee ingenuity and individual heroics. They are perfecting the spacecraft of the future. Project Mercury, by contrast, is portrayed as bureaucratic and slapdash, a publicity stunt designed to show the world that America still held the technological high ground.

This "quick and dirty" mobilization of scientific and engineering resources was politically astute enough to work, Wolfe argues, so long as the human component, the astronaut, could be celebrated. Even the candidates for astronaut volunteering for the program seemed unconcerned about the shift from aerodynamic to ballistic status until they understood the full implication of their passive roles. The astronaut/protagonist was really nothing more than a test subject at best in the original conception of Project Mercury. Attached to biomedical sensors and strapped passively into a fully automated capsule sealed from the outside, the astronaut was literally just along for the ride.

This passivity was counterintuitive to what the worried post-*Sputnik* masses needed in the way of American heroes, however, so NASA emphasized their military records as elite pilots and sold that version to the media. It succeeded beyond NASA's narrow need to win the hearts and minds of the taxpayer:

> Without exception, the newspapers and wire reports picked out the highlights of their careers and carefully massed them to create a single blaze of glory. . . . All seven, collectively, emerged in a golden haze as the seven finest pilots and bravest men in the United States. A blazing aura was upon them all.
>
> It was if the press in America, for all its vaunted independence, were a great colonial animal, an animal made up of countless clustered organisms responding to a single nervous system. In the late 1950's (as in the late 1970's) the animal seemed determined that in all matters of national importance the *proper emotion,* the *seemly sentiment,* the *fitting moral tone* should be established and should prevail; and all information that muddied the tone and weakened the feeling should be thrown down the memory hole. (121–22)

The glorification of the astronauts had really gotten out of hand! In the world of science—and Project Mercury was supposed to be a scientific enterprise—pure scientists ranked first and engineers ranked second and the test-subjects of experiments ranked so low that one seldom thought about them. But here the test subjects . . . were national heroes! They created a zone of awe and reverence wherever they set foot! Everyone else, whether physicist, biologist, doctor, psychiatrist, or engineer, was a mere attendant. (179)

The inner voice here is that of an engineer reacting to the inversion of power created by the press. Wolfe is using this novelistic license to stress the power of image making that throughout much of *The Right Stuff* provides the context for a less sanitized version of actual events. The enormous risks and spectacular failures of Project Mercury in its early stages are shaped into palatable accounts by the popular press. *Life* magazine is the "fraternity bulletin of the Mercury astronauts" (210) at a time when none of them has even left the ground, while X-15 pilot Bob White has flown 136,500 feet (25 plus miles) into space. Though that feat gets him a *Life* cover, it does little to counterbalance the shift of emphasis to the astronauts.

Even the notorious failures of early unmanned rocket flights were recast in the popular press to read as though they were moderate successes. One notorious example is the account of the test launch of the first operational Mercury-Redstone rocket on November 21, 1960. The MR-1, as it was called, aborted its firing sequence one second into its launch when two power plugs disengaged twenty milliseconds apart rather than simultaneously as they were designed to do. The computer read that as a malfunction and shut down the main engines while launching the escape tower of the Mercury capsule as programmed. John Glenn's ghostwritten account of this episode in *We Seven* is typical: "Some humorists at the Cape referred to this first test of MR-1 as 'the day we launched the escape tower.' Actually, it was a more noteworthy day than that. Once we realized that the capsule had made the best of a confusing situation and had gone on to perform its duties just as it would have on a normal flight, we were rather proud of it. It had omitted only one step, as a matter of fact."[8] Glenn's emphasis on the performance of the capsule and his nearly total lack of discussion about the failure of the Redstone booster reflect his privileged frame of reference. To the astronaut/engineer/scientist enclave, the sealed-off space inside the capsule *is* the mission. The booster is nearly extraneous: gunpowder in a barrel.

Tom Wolfe's account in *The Right Stuff* is less charitable, adopting the tone and point of view of a dignitary brought in to witness the dress rehearsal for America's first manned launch. The object of this representative of the taxpaying public's gaze is the gleaming rocket that promises to erupt in fire and power and thunder its way aloft. Absent is any pretense of the scientific method, which often learns as much or more by failures than by success. Instead, we have the attitude of image-conscious Cold War politicians:

> They flew five hundred VIPs, including many congressmen and prominent Democrats, down to the Cape for the big event. . . . Everything except an astronaut was on the launch pad. The dignitaries were all seated in grandstands, and the countdown was intoned over the public address system: "Nine . . . eight . . . seven . . . six . . ." and so forth, and then: "We have ignition" . . . and the mighty belch of flames bursts out of the rocket in a tremendous show of power. . . . The mighty white shaft rumbles and seems to bestir itself—and then seems to change its mind, its computerized central nervous system, about the whole thing, because the flames suddenly cut off, and the rocket settles back down on the pad, and there's a little *pop*. The cap on the tip of the rocket comes off. It goes shooting up in the air, a tiny thing with a needle nose. In fact, it's the capsule's escape tower. As the great crowd watches, stone silent and befuddled, it goes up to about 4,000 feet and descends under a parachute. It looks like a party favor. . . . Five hundred VIPs had come all the way to Florida . . . to see the fires of Armageddon and hear the earth shake with the thunder—and instead they get this . . . this *pop* . . . and a cork pops out of a bottle of Spumante. (207)

This is the (imagined) indignant response of the spectator, someone who has quite literally come to view a spectacle and who has come away disappointed. From the grandstand point of view the launch is a monumental flop; it doesn't even offer the consolation prize of a midair explosion.

But in the skilled hands of a writer who has cast off the artificial restraints of "objectivity" and pushed his concept of "New Journalism" to the edges of its own stylistic space, a failure like that of MR-1 is another site for literary exploration. The emerging rhetorical power of documentary journalism provides Wolfe, as it had provided Mailer, with something that the traditional novel form had always tried to disguise, the opportunity to historicize using the narrative techniques of fiction while holding to the facticity of the actual event. Dialogue, status details, and scene-by-scene construction could be combined with documentary research to plot out the events of recent history in vivid dramatic detail. In a sense, getting the story became the story. In Mailer's case he was still the major player in his drama to decide if it will be possible to recover the enormous complexity of the lunar landing and save it from the rational syntax of science.

For Wolfe the story is the complicity of *Life* magazine and network television in scripting the astronauts into the ideal American heroes of an Eisenhower age so his project is to recover the suppressed history of the space program. *The Right Stuff* is, as Chris Anderson notes, "an investigation of language on many levels . . . the rhetoric of politicians . . . the rhetoric of press . . . the rhetoric of the astronauts themselves."[9] Wolfe's formal training in American Studies (Ph.D., Yale, 1957) and years as a journalist serve him well in his treatment of press and politicians, but the astronauts pose a unique problem. As he has with so many of his previous subjects in *The Kandy-Kolored Tangerine-Flake Streamline Baby, The Pumphouse Gang,* and *The Electric Kool Aid Acid Test,* Wolfe is once again trying to put into words an experience that strains the limits of traditional discourse. And even as he does it he reinforces his role

as outsider because to translate the ineffable quality of the experience into language is to set himself apart from the practitioners—
in this case, the test pilots. He cannot do much more than retell
the stories that the astronauts have told him, but he can use the
syntactic and stylistic skills of his own special training to swoop
and dazzle.

To examine this shaping power of representation, Wolfe adopts
a point of view that is not quite so familiar as the second-person
plural of his *Rolling Stone* articles but shares that sense of intimate
closeness. He often shifts between a certain expository distance
and the privileged subjectivity of first-person narration: "In the
training film the flight deck was a grand piece of gray geometry,
perilous, to be sure, but an amazing abstract shape as one looks
down upon it on the screen. And yet once the newcomer's two feet
were on it . . . *Geometry*—my God, man, this is a . . . skillet!"
(26) The intent here, as throughout the book, is to express the
ineffable, the sublime, experience that cannot be put into words.
Flying in general, and test piloting or becoming an astronaut in
particular, are experiences so physically and psychically removed
from general experience that no common vocabulary seems to exist
to mediate them. But mediate them Wolfe must or he has no book
so he situates his narrative voice within the circumscribed space of
these pilots but just short of the pilots themselves. Instead of the
stylistic excess of his *Rolling Stone* article ("Heeeeee—yuh—yuh—
yuh—yuh—yuh—yuh—yuh we're not laughing at you, Tom. It's
just that the question you're asking always used to be such a joke
with us. . . . Nobody ever *has* described what we experienced."), he
begins *The Right Stuff* by evoking a side of the class, gender, and
race triad. The first chapter, "The Angels," begins:

> Within five minutes, or ten minutes, no more than that,
> three of the others had called her on the telephone to ask her
> if she had heard that something had happened out there.
> "Jane, this is Alice. Listen, I just got a call from Betty, and

she said she heard something's happened out there. Have you heard anything?" That was the way they phrased it, call after call. She picked up the telephone and began relaying this same message to some of the others.

"Connie, this is Jane Conrad. Alice just called me, and she says something's happened. . . ."

Something was official Wife Lingo for tiptoeing blindfolded around the subject.(3)

The rapidity with which the phone calls come in, the sense of urgency, the obvious connection between the consequences of whatever has happened and the somebody who progresses from "her" to "Jane" to "Jane Conrad" all carry the reader into the narrative in the same way an effective periodic sentence can create tension by suspending closure. The tone and point of view are those of individuals clearly on the periphery of actions that affect them but over which they have no control.

The telephone connects them; they speak a code; they call not to inquire but to announce. They are women—in this case the wives of navy pilots, but it will be the same for the astronauts' wives—and the domestic space they inhabit is contained within the grid of an incredibly complex military structure. They provide Wolfe precisely that privileged point of view he needs for his counterhistory of Project Mercury because, on the whole, military wives represent the best example of decentered subjects available in our society. After all, they are not, technically, in the service themselves, yet they are definitely part of the organizational structure when it comes to protocol and to assisting their husbands' ascent along the pyramid of rank. Officers' wives are invested with power and privilege commensurate with their husbands' rank and are not generally thought of beyond that context.

By shifting away from the sardonic egocentricity of the astronauts themselves and selecting instead Jane Conrad, wife of astronaut Pete Conrad, as his point-of-view character, Wolfe is able to pinpoint the structural weakness of a system that takes an intelligent Bryn Mawr graduate and relegates her to a state of powerlessness. The key structural weakness, to Wolfe at least, is the inability of NASA to comprehend fully the linguistic force of what NASA thinks is rational engineering.

The "something" that has happened is, we discover, the crash of an aircraft and very likely the death of one of their husbands. The wives cannot speak in terms so final so they speak in euphemisms and by telephone, each waiting helplessly to hear her husband's voice telling her that he is okay. The announcer of death will certainly be male. A fellow officer and a chaplain will deliver the bad news personally at the door.

All in all, Wolfe uses "The Angels" to set up his central trope of test pilots/astronauts as a special breed—the latest incarnation of the solo warrior, the distillate of a thousand deaths—so set apart from all others, including their wives, that they can communicate effectively only with each other. By beginning from Jane Conrad's point of view and showing her fundamental inability to share in her husband's experience of flying, Wolfe is able to personify his dilemma of trying to write a narrative that resists its telling because of its ineffable nature. "He couldn't explain it. After all, the very words for it had been amputated. . . . By this point, a young fighter jock was like the preacher in *Moby Dick* who climbs up into the pulpit on a rope ladder and then pulls the ladder up behind him; except the pilot could not use the words necessary to express the vital lessons" (34).

By decentering the narrative and showing the world of experimental aviation through the eyes of an affected party, Jane Conrad, Wolfe also gives the reader a place to "stand," more or less. We are continually presented first with banal language that has reduced the horror of death to phrases like "something happened," "he bought it today," and "burned beyond recognition." Then, once the euphe-

misms have taken hold and the danger made routine, Wolfe shifts
gears and attempts a full descriptive impact of what a fatal crash
looks, sounds, and smells like:

> "Burned beyond recognition" . . . was quite an artful euphe-
> mism to describe a human body that now looked like an enor-
> mous fowl that has burned up in a stove, burned a blackish
> brown all over, greasy and blistered, fried, in a word, with
> not only the entire face and all the hair and the ears burned
> off, not to mention all the clothing, but also the *hands* and
> *feet,* with what remains of the arms and legs bent at the knees
> and elbows and burned into absolutely rigid angles, burned a
> greasy blackish brown like the bursting body itself. (5)

Through multiple anecdotes of fatal mishaps the reader gradually understands the powerless perspective of Jane Conrad and just
what it means to say that test pilots have a 23 percent mortality
rate. To have lived with the knowledge that your husband chose
willingly to pursue a career that gave you a one-in-four chance of
being a widow before age thirty results finally in a certain fatalism.
Wolfe uses this fatalism to bridge into his history of Project Mercury and the suppressed history of the X-series tests by focusing
on his own particular adversary, the popular press he refers to as
that "Victorian Gent":

> She now knew the subject and the essence of this enterprise,
> even though not a word of it had passed anybody's lips. . . .
> Seven years later, when a reporter and photographer from
> *Life* magazine actually stood near her in her living room and
> watched her face, while outside, on the lawn, a crowd of tele-
> vision crewmen and newspaper reporters waited for . . . for
> some sign of what she felt . . . it made Jane want to laugh, but
> in fact she couldn't even manage a smile.
>
> Why ask *now?* she wanted to say. But they wouldn't have
> had the faintest notion of what she was talking about. (20)

And that is, after all, the tension of *The Right Stuff*—how to give the reader some notion of what these test pilots are talking about. This is important not so much because Wolfe wants to lionize the individual heroics of astronauts and test pilots but because of what they represented on the American landscape of the 1970s. It becomes a narrative of cultural empowerment—Henry Luce's efforts to shape the manned space program into a "Presbyterian vision" of American election—that can be undercut only by an equally stereotypical American narrative—Wolfe's conception of astronauts as mavericks out West.

The Right Stuff moves through three levels of mediated representation: (1) the domestic space of the astronauts' wives; (2) the narrative imagination of the astronauts' perspective, with all its attendant demographics no longer linked to the composite created by the popular press; and (3) the privileged space of the journalists, which, however removed from the real players, is still closer than where the public stands and directly responsible for the distance between them.

This is also roughly the organization of the book. After "The Angels" and "The Right Stuff," which is Wolfe's most metadiscursive chapter, the central chapters trace the technical history of Project Mercury by chronicling the astronaut's journey from "lab rat" to "spacecraft pilot" within the narrow fraternity of test pilots themselves. Since the distinction, however unsubtle, was never important to the adoring public, Wolfe is primarily concerned with writing a behind-the-scenes drama of actual and rhetorical competition between test pilots and astronauts. The complicity of the media to elevate one and nearly ignore the other is a major subtext. Irreverent narratives of the first three Mercury flights, Alan Shephard's, Gus Grissom's, and John Glenn's, are all recast in the light of a Cold War space race which doomed the scientific nature of the missions in favor of demonstrations of engineering triumphs.

From Wolfe's perspective, the great shining moment of America's love affair with space is John Glenn's three-orbit mission.

He is met by the president when he returns to Cape Canaveral; he is awarded the Medal of Freedom at a White House ceremony; and he and the other six astronauts are paraded through New York City on a scale more triumphant than the greeting Charles Lindbergh received. As it has for Bellow, Updike, and Mailer, New York looms large on the terrain of American cultural history; the astronauts' parade functions as an appropriate descriptive closure for the astronauts' ascendancy to the top of the pyramid of the right stuff:

> Despite the tide of cheers and tears that had already started in Washington none of them knew what to expect in New York. Like most military people . . . they didn't really consider New York part of the United States. It was like a free port, a stateless city, an international protectorate, Danzig in the Polish corridor. . . . It was a foreign city full of a strange race of curiously tiny malformed gray people. . . . What they saw when they got there bowled them over. The crowds were not only waiting in the airport, . . . but they were also lining the godforsaken highway into the city, . . . out in the freezing cold in the most rancid broken-down industrial terrain you have ever seen, a decaying landscape that seemed to belong to another century—they were out there *along the highway,* anywhere they could squeeze in, and . . . they were crying! (346–47)

According to Wolfe, from that moment on Project Mercury became a victim of its own success. Subsequent flights captured the public attention briefly, but they were, after all, repetitions of a spectacle already witnessed. Only the engineering triumphs distinguished one flight from another, and that is not the stuff of charisma to the media or to the general public. But paradoxically, it is precisely the missing ingredient that reintegrates the astronaut experience with the test-pilot experience.

Wolfe's last three chapters, "The Operational Stuff," "The Club," and "The High Desert," mark the permanent ascendancy

of astronauts to the top of the pyramid almost in direct propor-
tion to their "fall from cowboy heaven" in the eyes of the media.
Cutbacks to the X-series program have finally put the astronauts
alone at the top, even in the eyes of the test pilots. The measure of
this is Wolfe's Epilogue, a neat chronicle of the events in 1963 that
marked the final bureaucratization of the right stuff. The threshold
of space had been officially defined by the air force as fifty miles up,
so two X-15 military pilots, Joe Walker and Bob Rushworth, were
awarded astronaut wings for flying that craft into space. The seven
Mercury astronauts were collectively awarded the highest honor
of the Society of Experimental Test Pilots, the Iven C. Kincheloe
Award, for outstanding professional performance in the conduct of
a flight test. During the summer of 1963 the U.S.-Soviet nuclear test
ban treaty and a ban on nuclear weapons in orbit were signed. The
famous "hotline" was installed between Moscow and Washington.
"The Cold War, as anyone could plainly see, was over" (435).

In the immediate years after the last Apollo flight in 1972, it
must have seemed to Wolfe's finely honed sense of American cultural history that Mailer's complaint—"The horror of the Twentieth
Century was the size of each new event, and the paucity of its re-
verberation"[10]—was correct. What might remain of the first stage of
America's Manned Space Program, in the collective consciousness
of the received history, would likely be Apollo 11's lunar landing.
The names and exploits of those who pioneered that technology—
the solo warriors who pushed the outside of the envelope—were in
danger of fading into footnotes. The Right Stuff and the subsequent
film adaptation, in their attempts to rewrite the Mercury program
in terms of the western, succeed not so much in recovering a more
heroic version of the astronauts but in recovering instead the lost
history of the test pilots at Edwards Air Force Base.

Just consider the other arena of space—what Mailer called
"vending Space"—as a measure of the enduring image of astronauts
and test pilots. The success of Wolfe's belated celebration of Yeager
and the X-series test pilots is nowhere more evident than in Yeager's

appeal for Madison Avenue. He has survived, even thrived on, the commodification of his image on television by the likes of General Motors although not one of the original astronauts, notably Wally Schirra and Scott Carpenter, has ever sounded convincing selling cold remedies or cars.[11] The ineffable quality of the right stuff is now purchasable at your nearest retail dealer.

The content and purpose of the war must be made clear to

the masses by means of propaganda. . . . Such propa-

ganda cannot possibly, however, restrict itself to

the individual, isolated war. It has to re-

veal the social content, the historical

presuppositions and circumstances of

the struggle, to connect up the war

with the entire life and possibilities of

the nation's development.—Georg Lukács, *The*

Historical Novel

Beyond simple steel erection, the Rocket was an entire

system won, *away from the feminine darkness, held*

against the entropies of loveable scatterbrained

Mother Nature. . . . By understanding the

Rocket, he would come to understand

truly his manhood.—Thomas

Pynchon, *Gravity's*

Rainbow

6

Chemistry and Colonialism Gone Ballistic:
Apprehending the Mass of *Gravity's Rainbow*

Few contrasts in visible authority could be greater than those between Mailer's style and Thomas Pynchon's. Mailer's presence as central character in *Of a Fire on the Moon,* despite the chapter's third-person voice and title claim of "A Loss of Ego," is indisputable from the first sentence—"Norman, born sign of Aquarius, had been in Mexico when the news came about Hemingway." He is always a brooding visible presence, not merely on the back cover of the dust jacket and throughout the work but publicly as well. Pynchon, by contrast, is invisible, as void of clear agency as the aurally passive "A screaming comes across the sky" that opens *Gravity's Rainbow.*

This need to be present only by way of the aftershock, the sonic boom of his latest literary passage, marks in Pynchon a very different conception of narrative and, in a sense, the world that is narrated. Like Tyrone Slothrop, "who was sent into the Zone to be present at his own assembly—perhaps . . . *his time's assembly*" but ended up "scattered" and lost to "centrifugal History," Thomas Pynchon has labored to disperse himself in such a way that he, too, is a disintegrated presence at his own time's assembly.[1] His "time" is twenty-five years later than the fictional setting of *Gravity's Rainbow;* his "time" is defined and destabilized by the synthetic power of corporate technique focused in the metonymy of the Rocket.

He has been a part of it. After his sophomore year at Cornell he interrupted his engineering studies to enlist in the navy. He returned to Cornell after two years to finish his degree in English. He worked for Boeing Aerospace Corporation from February 1960 to September 1962 as an "engineering aide" developing technical documents on the Minuteman solid-fuel ICBM—to this day one of the mainstays of the United States's nuclear strike capability.[2]

Where, for Mailer (and even more so for Wolfe, Updike, and Bellow) power is still situated in some nexus of government and business and only its application for good or evil is in question, power for Pynchon has become, or perhaps has always been, some protean force slipped beyond the specific site of any leveling bureaucracy. "All talk of cause and effect is secular history, and secular history is a diversionary tactic," says a voice that might or might not be the ghost of Walter Rathenau speaking through a medium. "You must ask two questions. First, what is the real nature of synthesis? And then: what is the real nature of control" (167).

Synthesis and *control* are key words in *Gravity's Rainbow.* Synthesis, in its most straightforward sense of "putting together," "combining parts to form a whole," is sufficient to speak to the encyclopedic structure of *Gravity's Rainbow,* but its other denotations relating to grammar, chemistry, physics, and philosophy are even closer to the center of Pynchon's concerns. In grammar it refers to the privileging of sense over strict syntax; in chemistry it is the production of a substance by the union of chemical elements, groups, or simpler compounds or by the degradation of a complex compound; in physics it refers to the production of white or other compound light by combination of its constituent colors; in Kantian philosophy synthesis denotes "the action of the understanding in combining and unifying the isolated data of sensation into a cognizable whole";[3] and in crude Hegelian terms it is a dialectic combination of thesis and antithesis into a higher form of truth.

Similarly, control carries with it not only the sense of power and restraint but also the scientific model of "controlled experiment"—judging effects by means of a parallel experiment in which subjects are treated identically, except that the procedure or agent under test is omitted. Add to this the definition of control as also the term for spirits who actuate the utterances of a medium in a seance and the word begins to inhabit both the empirical and the irrational worlds.

Pynchon's technique in *Gravity's Rainbow* is not unlike that of an organic chemist running experiments with blind controls on the synthesis of new compounds. Combined in bizarre ways, the flow of information in the novel structurally reproduces the cognitive challenge presented by a world as informationally complex and relative as ours has become. Like the world around us, *Gravity's Rainbow* bombards us with data—science, religion, government jargon, mysticism, music, political history, economics, slang—with no attempt to prioritize, or foreground, those that are significant from those that are background. What the novel of social realism would have used as a historical frame for its characters, Pynchon deploys as a zone of reference whose boundaries are as fluid, overlapping, and interpenetrating as syntax will allow. The reader, searching for clues to priority, selects those incidents and images that conform to his or her own preexisting private narrative and thereby situate the novel inside a received history. Weissman's final words to Gottfried—"there are ways of getting back, but so complicated, so at the mercy of language"—represent the whole problem of history and *Gravity's Rainbow*.

And yet, despite this effort to subvert the linguistic ordering of history inherent in any narrative, Pynchon's work does have a tacit chronometric to it. Like the long weekend that contains the events of *Mr. Sammler's Planet,* the four-month span of *Rabbit Redux,* the six-month time frame of *Of a Fire on the Moon,* and the first decade of the Space Age in *The Right Stuff,* the chronological narrative of *Gravity's Rainbow* is roughly the last nine months of World War II,

December 1944 to September 1945. But the work is so filled with analepsis and prolepsis that any fixed sense of time and place is unstable more often than not.

What is relatively stable, though extratextual, is the synchrony of its production. *Gravity's Rainbow* is indisputably a product of all the social upheaval in the 1960s and can be read as countermemory, an effort by Pynchon to trace the genealogy of that unrest back to certain failings of colonialism in the seventeenth and the early twentieth centuries.

This historicity of the novel is, I think, one of the most appealing parts of a work that is as filled with components as the V-2 rocket that serves as its central trope. The moment in which Pynchon wrote *Gravity's Rainbow* was the moment of America's triumph in space and America's disaster in Vietnam. The print and electronic media were filled with daily accounts of both fiery liftoffs from Cape Canaveral and firefights from Southeast Asia. Pynchon's own brief tenure with Boeing was but recent memory. He had published *V* (1963) and *The Crying of Lot 49* (1966), two novels of institutional paranoia in postmodern America, and had tried to chart the troubled waters of racial unrest in "A Journey into the Mind of Watts," an article for the *New York Times Magazine* (1966).

Pynchon is reported to have begun a version of *Gravity's Rainbow* from ideas he had when writing *V* but put it aside to work on *The Crying of Lot 49* before returning to complete the first draft, appropriately enough, on engineer's quadrille paper.[4] Assuming the period between 1967 and 1972 as the gestational period for the novel, the litany of global and domestic upheaval that bombarded the airwaves would have had to find its way into the work. Little wonder, then, that what was finally published on February 18, 1973, can be read as a jeremiad couched in the form of a postmodernist historical fiction whose real subject is the very status of history.

Though some of the most creative and fruitful approaches to *Gravity's Rainbow* have been through its use of history, no one seems to have examined its status as a postmodern version of the historical novel.[5] Georg Lukács, in *The Historical Novel,* ends with a subchapter titled "Prospects of Development for the New Humanism in the Historical Novel," which makes the claim that the

> historical novel of today gives only an *abstract prehistory of ideas* and not the concrete prehistory of the people themselves, which is what the historical novel in its classical period portrayed.
>
> As a result of this general and conceptual rather than concrete and historical relationship between past and present the distortion of historical figures or movements is at times inevitable; there is thus a falling away from that superb faithfulness to historical reality. . . . The direct and conceptual relationship with the present which prevails today reveals an immanent tendency to turn the past into a *parable of the present.*[6]

Lukács is not calling for a return of the historical novel to the political work done by Scott and Cooper in their novels of the "middle course" that emerges from the violent "progress" of historical crises. He does not want a fiction of consolation that rationalizes the way things are but rather a recovery of art's ability to be a popular arbiter of social change. Pynchon would probably dispute this possibility, but *Gravity's Rainbow* is, at the very least, a text that finds the shape of his world formed by the Potsdam Conference in much the same way that Scott located his in the battle of Culloden.

Had Lukács known of the curious application of this recovery of the historical novel by American novelists bent on dismantling the monolithic master narrative of World War II that had the United States riding nobly to the defense of embattled Europe and Russia, he might have been heartened. The anti-Nazi German fiction that he had celebrated in 1937 could not prevent the devastation of Europe, but once the Wermacht dragon was slain, the literature, film, television scripts, and histories that were written over the next twenty years sealed the war hermetically inside a simplistic struggle of Cold War good and evil. The Allies (read Americans) "liberated" the German people (particularly rocket scientists) from Nazi atrocities without ever committing any themselves, while the brutal Russians "captured" other hapless scientists and all of Eastern Europe.

About the time the Soviet space triumphs of the late 1950s and early 1960s began to shake the credibility of official stories, a new generation of war novels also appeared. It was almost as if the erosion of Eisenhower's influence on the decade signaled a permission to reconsider the war itself. Joseph Heller's *Catch 22* (1961) grounds the war in corporate greed by contrasting the media's interest in good stories and the multinational self-protection of companies like General Motors with the fragile terror of young American bomber pilots protecting those interests. Kurt Vonnegut's *Slaughterhouse Five* (1968) is his successful second attempt (he shies away from it in *Sirens of Titan* [1959]) to recover the suppressed history of the Allied firebombing of Dresden, which killed more than 140,000 civilians and totally destroyed the city. And Pynchon's first novel, *V,* also questions the socially mediated nature of any historical narrative.

By treating written history as selectively distorted and interest-bound, these new novels inverted the concept of the historical novel as a means by which a culture justifies the necessity of a violent past in order to bring about a more settled present. The parable of the present that emerges in these narratives is that of an incomprehensible grid of interpenetrating power running from corporation to government to military to media to school to home. Paranoia and distrust of the "official story" have become so ingrained after the Warren Commission, the Gulf of Tonkin incident, the Chicago Convention, and countless other obfuscations that the issue for writers in the 1960s was not how historical representations selectively distort the past but, rather, how these distortions function hegemonically to control present historical consciousness.

This paranoia is at the heart of *Gravity's Rainbow*. As Raymond Mazurek has observed, "Again and again, Pynchon associates the placing of the events within history with systems of deception, co-ercion, destruction."[7] History is a convenient fiction put in place by "Them," the elusive powerful who control the events of the world in part by adhering to "Proverbs for Paranoics, 3: If they can get you asking the wrong questions, they don't have to worry about answers" (251). Or, failing in that, the chronicling of events can be hegemonic: "The mass nature of wartime death is useful in many ways. It serves as spectacle, as diversion from the real movements of the War. It provides raw material to be recorded into History, so that children may be taught History as sequences of violence, battle after battle, and be more prepared for the adult world" (105).

To subvert the power of history-making Pynchon has created a novel that is, itself, not so much unmappable as multiply map-pable. Through its encyclopedic borrowing from myth, travelogue, history, science, medicine, religion, the popular press, and music, *Gravity's Rainbow* emerges as a counterhistory of all the doomed colonialist enterprises that culminated in World War II.

Brian Stonehill sees the novel as divided between a vision of a world that is "causal" (containing massive conspiracies) and a vision of a world that is "casual" (containing massive coincidences).[8] The "They" who make up PISCES, the White Visitation where Pavlovi-ans like Pointsman work, the chemical cartels like IG Farben, Shell Oil, and on and on, seem to Slothrop's mind evidence that, despite the apparent random Poisson distribution of his sexual conquests and the subsequent V-2 strikes, large forces control even the most private areas of individual lives. But, on the other hand, if those of the Counterforce, the preterite like Tyrone Slothrop, Roger Mexico, and Oberst Enzian who resist the forces of control by taking ad-vantage of the chaos and uncertainty of the Zone, can be seen as acting autonomously, then all the apparent links are made only by the paranoid tendencies of the characters (or the reader).

Of all the paranoiac historical plots in *Gravity's Rainbow* the best one that can be read as Lukács's "parable of the present," the one that perpetuates the privilege of the spatial over the temporal in contemporary narrative, is Pynchon's account of Kekulé's dream of the benzene ring.

The received account goes something like this: Friedrich August Kekulé von Stradonitz entered the University of Giessen as an architecture student with the aptitude for seeing the multiple dimensions of a structure graphed out on paper, then engineered into actual physical space. At the university he was influenced by the famous organic chemist Justus von Liebig to change his field to chemistry. Kekulé is reported to have envisioned the carbon ring structure of benzene molecules after a dream about a giant serpent devouring its own tail:

> He was stumped when he got to benzene. He knew there were six carbon atoms with a hydrogen attached to each one—but he could not see the shape. Not until the dream; until he was made to see it, so that others might be seduced by its physical beauty, and begin to think of it as a blueprint, a basis for new compounds, new arrangements, so that there would be a field of aromatic chemistry to ally itself with secular power, and find new methods of synthesis, so there would be a German dye industry to become the IG. (412)

The IG is, of course, the Interessen Gemeinschaft Farbenindustrie Aktiengesellschaft (Dye Industry Community of Interests, Incorporated), or, IG Farben, the massive chemical, drug, synthetic fiber, rubber, film, and dye cartel whose multinational power and influence are so extensive and obscure that it serves Pynchon as the best example of the death-seeking, bureaucratic "Firm" whose market interests were served by World War II at the expense of literally millions of small lives. Kekulé's discovery of the hexagonal carbon bond is the foundation of aromatic chemistry, the birth of all products derived from petroleum—high-octane fuels, polymer plastics, even some pharmaceuticals. The oneiric nature of his discovery sets the tone for its industrial implications. From a waste product of steel manufacturing—coal tar—a new industry is created, new compounds are synthesized, and then some market for that product is created, "to be delivered into a system whose only aim is to *violate* the Cycle. Taking and not giving back, demanding that 'productivity' and 'earnings' keep on increasing with time, the System removing from the rest of the World these vast quantities of energy to keep its own tiny desperate fraction showing a profit" (412).

The entropic toll taken on the world by this new chemical industry and its colonial drain of human and mineral resources are as close as *Gravity's Rainbow* comes to having a thematic center. Like the repetitive chaining of polymers made possible by understanding the benzene structure, the looping asymmetrical plots that orbit the mass of Pynchon's encyclopedic novel are as enigmatic and seductive as the Imipolex G that Slothrop seeks. At one point or another, all the plots pass through remote and empty spaces, Puritan America and Dutch Mauritius in the seventeenth century, German Southwest Africa and Argentina in the nineteenth century, and Soviet Kirghiztan in the twentieth century. They are the mineral-rich places on maps, colonized places on maps, genocidal places on maps.

The Kekulé anecdote is the best example. Pynchon writes it into his novel as part of an elaborate description of pre-Hitler Berlin, circa 1929–30. Berlin is depicted as a place for occultists, dreaming engineers interested in rockets, visionary filmmakers such as Fritz Lang (*Die Frau im Mond*), and anxious revolutionaries.

The story is related by Professor Lazlo Jamf to Franz Pökler in the course of a chemistry seminar he is taking during his studies. Jamf is the elusive, peripatetic chemical genius of IG Farben who may have conducted bizarre conditioning experiments on Tyrone Slothrop as a child. Franz Pökler is one of the typical chemical engineers working on rockets before World War II who will be pressed into service by the Nazis to build V-2s. And in the primary and secondary settings of our own reading of *Gravity's Rainbow* and Pökler's prewar Germany we have a double perspective of how the dream of 1865 has been enlarged by research and industrial expansion to reach a critical mass that affects the lives of the entire planet from World War II forward. As Scott Sanders has noted, "We are presented not with a plot of interwoven fates, but with overlapping case histories of private manias, each character locked into his or her own conspiratorial fantasy."[9]

All the sympathetic characters, Slothrop, Mexico, Katje, Enzian, Tchitcherine, are given histories that have their genealogy in colonialist enterprises. Slothrop is a descendant of a Puritan heretic of the Massachusetts Bay Colony; Mexico, if nothing else, carries the name of a succession of empire dreams from Cortés to Maximilian; Borgesius has ties through her ancestors to Belgian attempts to colonize Mauritius; Tchitcherine's life is linked to failed czarist dreams of conquest that died in the Sino-Russian War; and the Herero, Enzian, is a consequence of both Russian and German imperialism in Southwest Africa.

The power of language to bring about what it utters is another version of the oneiric impulse. The benzene structure is dreamed and, from it, "plasticity's central canon: that chemists were no longer to be at the mercy of Nature" (249). Rockets are envisioned by Jules Verne, H. G. Wells, and Fritz Lang, then made operational by engineers who believe the fiction. Schwarzkommandos are dreamed up by Psy-Ops, then discovered to be real, and so on. Nowhere in *Gravity's Rainbow* is this more dramatically narrated than in the Kirghiz Light episode involving Vaslav Tchitcherine.

As Pynchon's Soviet version of the Cold War narrative, Tchitcherine, the oft-wounded ("more metal than anything else") Technical Intelligence officer is Slothrop's Russian counterpart in the Zone. Officially, his mission is also to gather the secrets (and the scientists) of the V-2 rocket for his country, but he has a private mission as well. He desires to kill Oberst Enzian, his Herero half-brother.

No summary can do justice to Pynchon's textual richness, but the gist of it is as follows. Tchitcherine's father, a gunner on board a Russian warship during the Sino-Russian War of 1904, impregnates a Herero woman during the ship's coaling stop in Southwest Africa. The elder Tchitcherine sails on to his death with the rest of the Russian fleet, leaving Vaslav in St. Petersburg and soon-to-be born Enzian in Lüderitzbucht. Years later, the younger Tchitcherine discovers his brother's existence from Berlin records he has access to after the Rapallo treaty (signed by Rathenau and an unrelated Tchitcherine) opens lines of trade between the two countries. Before he can act on the information, he is transferred to the Central Asian frontier province of Kazahstan in reprisal for an illicit affair. There he is to be part of the Soviet government's effort to develop its own oil industry while simultaneously consolidating the revolution through centralized literacy programs.

Charged with supplanting the oral Arabic culture of the Kirghiz with a written one based on the New Turkish Alphabet, Tchitcherine is part of a social experiment that exploits the political use of language. This account of the reduction of the Kirghiz people's language of orality, a language that was "purely speech, gesture, touch" (338), allows Pynchon to explore what Edward Mendelson sees as the ideological center of *Gravity's Rainbow,* "the transformation of charismatic energy into the controlled and rationalized routine of a bureaucracy." [10]

As the best example of Max Weber's twice-cited "routinization of charisma" (325, 364), the Kirghiz Light episode dramatizes the fleeting instability of authority based on the ideal of love and brotherhood. Though it may flourish briefly during the decline of dynastic power, in fact can flourish only in moments of extreme disruption, charismatic authority soon falls victim to the bureaucratic necessity of administering power and becomes abstract and impersonal. [11]

The local folk culture is at the mercy of committees and subcommittees charged with standardizing an alphabet, transcribing the local dialects into print, and training native printers to publish and educate the population. The unanticipated power of this transformation of culture by politically imposed language is wonderfully compressed by Pynchon: "On sidewalks and walls the very first printed slogans start to show up, the first Central Asian fuck you signs, the first kill-the-police-commissioner signs (and somebody does! this alphabet is really something!) and so the magic that the shamans, out in the wind, have always known, begins to operate now in a political way" (355–56).

The Kirghiz Light episode also extends the parallel between synthesizing fuels for the engines of imperialism and synthesizing pharmaceutical compounds that alter the trajectory of human pain and perception. IG Farben's agent in Central Asia is Wimpe, the "V-man" (industrial spy) who was present, along with Pökler, Weissman, Enzian, and others, in an earlier episode, the seance in Munich circa 1930 at which the ghost of Walter Rathenau ties recent history to the rise of organic chemistry. Wimpe's major interest is the power of opium alkaloids and their analgesic/addictive vectors. Oil and opium in undeveloped Central Asia, Stalin and IG Farben, pain and deliverance, Tchitcherine and Wimpe all come together in Wimpe's reaction to Tchitcherine's assertion that drug companies are trafficking in profit, pain, and addiction: "We . . . believe in real pain, real deliverance—we are knights in the service of that Ideal. It must all be real for the purposes of our market. Otherwise my employer—*and our little chemical cartel is the model for the very structure of nations*—becomes lost in illusion and dream, and one day vanishes into chaos" (349, emphasis added). There is more than an eerie coincidence between Pynchon's lines and a memo written by NASA administrator James E. Webb in 1965 to presidential adviser Horace Busby: "Now what this may mean is that the government-industry-university team we have developed under the NASA system, which has been so effective in marrying science and technology and mobilizing large resources for focusing on limited but important objectives, might become the pattern needed by this nation."[12]

Shortly thereafter, Wimpe is transferred to the Chemnyco affiliate of IG Farben in New York to work with Lazlo Jamf. The legacy he has left Tchitcherine and readers of *Gravity's Rainbow* is that of the mythical oneirine theophosphate—a hallucinatory drug of dreams indicating the presence of God—whose dominant side effect is paranoia, "nothing less than the onset, the leading edge, of the discovery that *everything is connected,* everything in the Creation" (703). For Tchitcherine it is the paranoia of a "Rocket-cartel": "A structure cutting across every agency human and paper that ever touched it. . . . A state begins to take form in the stateless German night, a State that spans oceans and surface politics, sovereign as the International or the Church of Rome, and the Rocket is its soul. IG Raketen. . . . He will never get further than the edge of this meta-cartel which has made itself known tonight, this Rocket-state whose border he cannot cross" (566).

Another who senses the presence of the Rocket state is Tyrone Slothrop: "There is in his history, and likely, God help him, in his dossier, a peculiar sensitivity to what is revealed in the sky" (26). Among the "gray, preterite masses" who move about the Zone, Slothrop shares a heritage closest to Pynchon's. He is first introduced to the reader as decentered object, the focus of covert surveillance by Allied intelligence units interested in his uncanny ability to anticipate V-2 strikes. Well before we meet Slothrop we know the chaotic disarray of his desk. The narrative soon shifts to his point of view, however, and much of the novel unfolds as a consequence of his efforts to assemble the secrets of the V-2 rocket into a coherent whole even as he is himself beginning to disintegrate as any sort of narratively cohesive subject.

These two antagonistic movements—the assembly of the rocket and the progressive scattering of Slothrop—recur often enough among the overlapping layers of intertextual discourse that are laid out for the reader to process that they function, at least for me, as a way of apprehending the mass if not the whole of *Gravity's Rainbow.* He is a character who has very possibly been "engineered" to become the apotheosis of the Rocket state.

The parallel between Slothrop's fictional genealogy and Pynchon's own ancestors is significant in this context. After Slothrop improbably saves Katje Borgesius from the equally improbable octopus, the reader is given a brief insight into the historical workings of Slothrop's mind: "So it is here, grouped on the beach with strangers, that voices begin to take on a touch of metal, each word a hard-edged clap, and the light though as bright as before, is less able to illuminate . . . it's a Puritan reflex of seeking other orders behind the visible, also known as paranoia, filtering in" (188).

This "Puritan reflex" is extensively developed both as Slothrop's personal history and as a fundamental impulse throughout the work. The clinical characteristics of paranoia that locate its debilitating effects in radical self-referentiality—in the belief that behind all the seeming chaos of this life there is an order to events and that that order is focused in all its sinister energy on the self—is this century's and this technocratic state's answer to Calvinism gone ballistic.

The external manipulation of events in Slothrop's life is no longer the hand of God but the work of economically interested forces. As he discovers on his quest for the "S-Gerat" and the secret of Imipolex G, Slothrop's life may have been controlled since infancy by the chemical cartel IG Farben through its operatives Lazlo Jamf and Lyle Bland. It is a never-quite-clear transaction, which cuts across the actual historical figures of Hugo Stinnes and Walter Rathenau and their role in rebuilding industrial Germany. Stinnes and Rathenau indirectly enabled formation of the first multinational corporations that created an inflationary spiral in post–World War I Germany and destroyed the Weimar economy.[13] In the plot of Gravity's Rainbow, the paper mill owned by Slothrop's father supplies the necessary paper to print the millions of devalued Deutschmarks. In some transaction that is never quite clear (relying as it does on Slothrop's suppressed memory), part of the deal involves infant Tyrone, whose Harvard education is purchased for him in return for conditioning experiments involving the plastic polymer Imipolex G.

The conspiracy Pynchon creates here is both centrifugal and centripetal. Centrifugally, what happens to Slothrop is, from his or the narrator's point of view, just the outer edge of an American culture set spinning on the wrong trajectory three centuries earlier. In a fairly faithful transposition of his own Puritan history, Pynchon gives Slothrop a genealogy that goes back to the Massachusetts Bay Colony. The actual William Pynchon (1590–1662) was one of the original signers of the Cambridge Agreement of 1629 and became the ordnance expert in charge of purchasing weapons for the colonists.[14] He is credited with establishing the villages of Roxbury and, later, Springfield, at that time the westernmost frontier.

In 1650 he wrote a tract, *The Meritorious Price of Our Redemption,* which, by arguing a technical point about whether Christ needed to suffer the full torment of Hell in order to discharge the debt of the elect and secure their place in heaven, called into question the doctrine of election itself.[15] Parodied as *On Preterition* in *Gravity's Rainbow,* the tract is branded heretical and burned in Boston because it

> argued holiness for these "second Sheep," without whom there'd be no elect. . . . What Jesus was for the elect, Judas Iscariot was for the Preterite. Everything in the Creation has its equal and opposite counterpart. Could he [Slothrop's Puritan ancestor William] have been the fork in the road America never took, the singular point she jumped the wrong way from? Suppose the Slothropite heresy had had the time to consolidate and prosper? Might there have been fewer crimes in the name of Jesus, and more mercy in the name of Judas Iscariot? It seems to Tyrone Slothrop that there might be a route back . . . maybe for a little while all the fences are down, one road as good as another, the whole space of the Zone

cleared, depolarized, and somewhere inside the waste of it a single set of coordinates from which to proceed, without elect, without preterite, without even nationality to fuck it up. (556)

Pynchon works the paradox of his own ancestry for all it's worth in this satire. The William Pynchon/Slothrop who purchased the technological firepower to colonize New England, who sat in capital judgment on two witchcraft trials, who extended the frontier and made his fortune trading with the indigenous preterite population, then writes a tract that subverts election and tries in its own small way to make a space for all those Calvinism would leave disintegrated. For this he is vilified as a heretic. In disgust, both historical and fictional characters sail back to England and die where they began.

As Pynchon was writing *Gravity's Rainbow,* the latest version of this narrative of Puritan colonization and historical suppression was being played out in Vietnam. Mailer's *Why Are We in Vietnam?* (1967) explored the figurative and literal impact of Puritan sensibility and technological firepower on the American psyche. D.J.'s narrative of hunting Alaskan bear by helicopter is symptomatic of the insanity of Vietnam: "That's where I want my power. Right there. Right then. Maybe a professional hunter takes pride in dropping an animal by picking him off in a vital spot—but I like the feeling that if I miss a vital area I still can count on the big impact knocking them down, killing them by the total impact, shock! it's like aerial bombardment in the last Big War."[16]

Beyond the nightly news on television the media was exerting its own visual impact. *Life* magazine's June 27, 1969, issue carried the pictures of all 242 soldiers killed the previous week in a statistical, high school yearbook–like tableau that anticipated the spatial power of the names on the Vietnam War Memorial. Michael Herr's articles in *Esquire* between 1968 and 1970 (later published as *Dispatches*) also attempted to recover denuded lives caught in the grip of bureaucratic euphemism. Herr's statement that "you couldn't use

standard methods to date the doom" sets up his centripetal sense
that we "might as well say that Vietnam was where the Trail of Tears
was headed all along, the turnaround point where it would touch
and come back to form a containing perimeter; might just as well
lay it on the proto-Gringos who found the New England woods too
raw and empty for their peace and filled them up with their own
imported devils."[17]

The technological colonization of America is a counterhistory
to the ones about freedom and manifest destiny, Pynchon's novel
would seem to say. Not *the* counterhistory, just another way of orga-
nizing the material. By the twentieth century, eight generations
of Slothrops have diminished the family fortune such that Tyrone
Slothrop's life is mortgaged to the rocket cartel. Speaking through
the experience of Slothrop and through Oberst Enzian, Pynchon's
narrator, if not Pynchon himself, probes not just the ethical limits
of World War II's technocratic historicity but that of Vietnam and
the space race as well:

> This war was never political at all, the politics was all the-
> atre, all just to keep the people distracted . . . secretly, it was
> being dictated instead by the needs of technology . . . by a con-
> spiracy between human beings and techniques, by something
> that needed the energy-burst of war. . . . The real crises were
> crises of allocation and priority, not among firms—it was only
> staged to look that way—but among the different Technolo-
> gies, Plastics, Electronics, Aircraft, and their needs which are
> understood only by the ruling elite. (521)

Slothrop's search, then, is for "a set of coordinates" within the
whole, clear, depolarized space of the Zone which might lead to
freedom. If he can take advantage of the interim chaos before the
"They" system reorganizes the bureaucracy in occupied Germany
he might yet be free. Slothrop, like the reader, comes to understand that "*everything* is some kind of plot" but that not all plots are

"polarized upon himself" (603). The key (and the cost) of freedom is to view the interplay of plots as if "there is no more History, no time-traveling capsule to find your way back to, only the lateness and the absence that fill a great railway shed after the capital has been evacuated . . . everything else has gone away or fallen silent . . . barn-swallow souls, fashioned of brown twilight, rise toward the white ceilings . . . they are unique to the Zone, they answer to the new Uncertainty" (303). Or to see the Zone as: "an enormous transit system . . . and that by riding each branch the proper distance, knowing when to transfer, keeping some state of minimum grace though it might often look like he's headed the wrong way, this network of all plots may yet carry him to freedom" (603).

But if we are to believe the narrator, this doesn't happen. Something goes wrong; Slothrop disintegrates, scatters, and is lost to the narrator and the novel, or never really existed in the first place, but whichever, is lost to history. Which is absolutely what he desires because then he cannot be appropriated into even the smallest part of some narrative of progress that might perpetuate the system's hegemony. Pynchon does with Slothrop what he has attempted with his own life—he lets him disappear from the view of the systemizers, cause-and-effecters, and image-creators and seem to have no existence at all because there is no way to represent him.

Gravity's Rainbow is, then, anything but apolitical, although it resists determining any single coherent historical narrative because that power to make the past the concrete prehistory of the present is what perpetuates ideological domination. It was not the theology of Puritanism that created the Rocket state out of which Pynchon writes; it was the Puritans' secular professions, the economic and scientific expertise they had channeled their energy and intellect into, then transferred with them to America because, as dissenters, traditional avenues of power—government, law, clergy—were denied them in England. Freed of restraint, technology's power of signs creates its New World.

Like the emerging science of chaos-theory, which demonstrates the incredibly complicated interrelationship of complex systems whose shape and direction are never entirely predictable because of their sensitive dependence on initial conditions that are always unknown to the researcher, the paranoia of *Gravity's Rainbow* is not the sinister sense of malevolent hands pulling strings, but rather a sense of incredibly subtle contingency. What Tchitcherine and Slothrop discover, or rather fail to discover but intuit, is that the fluid dynamic of the Zone is not so much a momentary power void as it is a turbulent flow of multiple forces at that point of mixture where no clear channel is yet defined. Germany in the summer of 1945 is an interim, like Boston in 1650, Giessen in 1865, Südwest Afrika in 1904, Munich in 1930, or Los Angeles circa 1972. The Rocket state will be synthesized into its agent-absent ever-powerful presence, but not for a while.

Weissman's launching of Gottfried ("God's peace") in the V-2 is precursor to all this. Though the crude technique exists for someone as death-driven as Weissman to engineer a manned launch out of a ballistic weapon (this is, after all, just what the American and Russian space programs will do fifteen years later), "this ascent will be betrayed to Gravity. But the Rocket engine, the deep cry of combustion that jars the soul, promises escape. The victim, in bondage to falling, rises on a promise, a prophecy, of Escape" (758).

Unlike Mailer, who ends in grudging admiration of the engineers who have "taken the Moon" with technique while the counter/culture/force played, Pynchon sees the complex pull of human gravity as too great. Pynchon's apocalyptic ending seems to locate the reader in the Orpheus Theater watching all that has transpired in *Gravity's Rainbow* as cinema: "The screen is a dim page spread before us, white and silent. The film has broken" (760) just at the last delta-*t* before mega-death strikes in the form of a nuclear missile. There is time yet to reach out to the person next to you or to sing part of William Slothrop's suppressed hymn to preterition but no way to reverse the Newtonian calculus that has engineered extinction.

Powerful events breed their own network

of inconsistencies. Loose ends, dead

ends, small mysteries of time

and space. Violence it-

self seems to cause a

warp in the texture of

things. There are jump

cuts, blank spaces, an instant in

which information leaps from one energy

level to another.—Don DeLillo,

"Human Moments in World

War III"

7

Terror in a Lonely Place: Anomie and Anomaly in *Ratner's Star*

In the early 1960s the economic boom created by the space race was so explosive that for a while it seemed the fifty miles of scrub palmetto and cattle range between Orlando and Cape Canaveral would be replaced by the sprawl of new construction. The zone between the Econolahatchee and St. Johns Rivers would become the domestic heart of high-tech Florida.

In the dream of the developers, engineers would pour out of their white, cinder-block ranch homes every morning and then divide neatly into two streams, one driving west to the aerospace contractors in Orlando, the other east to the launch complex at Cape Canaveral.[1]

One visionary went so far as to purchase a large tract of land halfway to the Cape, just off the 528 bypass. He subdivided it into lots, paved the streets, put down curbing, even built a half dozen homes on speculation, and without a trace of irony named it Rocket City. Six homes, green lawns already turning yellow, shimmering in the refracted heat of a curving grid of new black asphalt. Not a tree anywhere. From the highway it resembled a withering oasis before it was even finished with Phase One. There would never be a Phase Two, at least in that decade, because the NASA cutbacks in personnel and contracts began in 1966 after the completion of

Project Gemini. Two or three of the houses were sold and for a while occupied by families stuck with houses that would never resell.

Once, on a hot, insect-droning afternoon on the way to Orlando with friends, I turned off into Rocket City. As we drove around the maze of streets covered by sand and windblown debris of palmetto fronds, pine needles, paper, and plastic, the place had the feel of one of those science fiction movies where an entire town has been wiped out by radiation.

In the distance, back where the boarded-up houses were sitting in sand, their lawns long lost, something low and mechanical was moving swiftly. As we approached, we saw that it was a go-cart, one of those homemade assemblages of wheels and steel tubing powered by a lawn mower engine no longer needed for its original purpose. A small sandy-haired boy was driving it flat out around a circuit of streets. He had done this often; the line of his constant circling had left the only clear track on the asphalt.

He didn't see us at first. We followed him about four car lengths behind for a lap and a half as, again and again, he dove into the apex of a corner, then allowed the acceleration and centrifugal force to carry him wide on the straightaway. The boy drove with the intensity and concentration of someone accustomed to playing alone.

At some point he must have sensed us or seen something coming out of one of the corners, maybe a glint of chrome, a shadow, or just the nape-tingling feeling that someone's watching, but whatever, he took his foot off the accelerator, drifted wide to the curb and looked back. What we must have looked like to him I can only imagine. Here in his abandoned world of streets, three grinning faces stared at him from a green '55 Ford. He couldn't have looked more frightened if we had been extraterrestrials.

We waved to him in feigned nonchalance and drove off laughing, leaving him to his paranoia. We never could tell which of the wasted homes must have housed him and his family. He was like some feral child of the technological age, living alone in the ruins.

Twenty years after the fact, I am coming to understand just how much all of us who grew up during that period, to a greater or lesser degree, lived in Rocket City no matter what our actual addresses. We were displaced persons, the sons and daughters of engineers brought to Cape Canaveral to build rockets. We all lived halfway between the actual geography of our families and the terra incognita of the present. We had grandparents who visited from places like Boston, Atlanta, and St. Louis and spoke of ancestral plots, graveyards full of relatives in cities we could barely place on a map. Meanwhile, our fathers fought against gravity, plotted different coordinates, and planned ways to take the next generation right off the map and into space.

As children the very games we invented were mixtures of the age-old and the new technology. We made mortars from the handlebars of our bicycles by inserting a firecracker in the hole of one plastic grip and wadded paper and a marble in the other open end of the handlebar tube. The explosion would toss the marble fifty yards or more. We made match-head rockets that cleared the neighbor's roof. We made mudballs out of the wet sand at the beach, but instead of throwing them at each other, we put live sand fiddlers inside and "launched" them to see how the fiddlers handled the stress of reentry. The lucky few who survived the first impact were launched again and again until they were crushed.

I did not, when I was young, have even the selective compassion for living creatures that I have as an adult. Ours was not the hardened view of death of country people who held back some part of themselves from children and animals because, after all, the world is a dangerous place and it doesn't do to get too attached too early. No, we were cruel in the way most children and some scientists are cruel. We wanted to discover something in our experiments about life and death, and though we didn't articulate it as such, the unspoken premise was that the animals were expendable because we were doing "research."

We were, all in all, somewhat average children of parents who were often exceptional. We played on the beaches while our fathers pushed science and technology to new limits. We viewed each triumph of technique as spectacular but not unexpected.

But what if we had been exceptional children of ordinary parents? What if just one of us had been so far beyond the norm that our ideas were comprehensible to only a few specialists in the world? What would the technocratic enterprise of NASA have seemed to us then?

This is, in an oblique way, Don DeLillo's point of departure in *Ratner's Star*. By extrapolating the contemporary state of scientific rationalism, with its penchant for abstraction, from the perspective of a fourteen-year-old mathematical genius named Billy Twillig, DeLillo's novel charts the power/knowledge grid of scientific research and its unresolvable impulse to seek absolutes among the endless proliferation of new data. It is, in a sense, a novel about the conflict between pure scientific method, with its interest in formulating hypotheses and acceptance of failed experiments, and technocracy, with its need to engineer solutions.

Billy Twillig is the son of "Babe" Terwilliger, a third-rail inspector in the New York subway system who believes that "existence is nourished from below, from the fear level, the plane of obsession, the starkest tract of awareness," and whose hobby is imitating batting stances of major leaguers.[2] DeLillo makes Billy's father a product of the modernist urban environment. Billy, like Albert Einstein, did not speak aloud until he was three. "His mind knew words. He spoke with his mind and to his mind" (69). His father is anxious to take him down into the tunnels of the subway system, "but not until he talks. I want to hear his reaction" (69). Billy's body resides in a grid space of the late Machine Age while his mind soars free in the topology of the Center for the Refinement of Ideational Structures, a mathematical think tank in Pennyfellow, Connecticut.

The physical action of *Ratner's Star* (what there is of it) is loosely arranged around Billy Twillig's journey to Field Experiment

Number One to decode a mathematical communication believed to originate from outer space. Sophisticated radio astronomy has picked up a signal of sufficient order and sequence to indicate the presence of extraterrestrial intelligence, but so far no one has been able to crack the code. As the first Nobel laureate in mathematics, Billy is expected to solve the mystery.

DeLillo is not writing directly about the space program in this novel, but his novel is certainly informed by its presence. Except for the 1975 Apollo-Soyuz rendezvous, there had been no manned American space activity since the end of the Skylab missions in 1973. The high-visibility phase was over for the moment. People now knew that despite the technical achievement of putting men on the moon, the current state of technology was completely inadequate to the equations of time and distance necessary for humans to travel even to the nearest planets, much less the nearest star. Waning public interest in the now seemingly routine spectacle of spaceflight and other economic considerations had greatly reduced NASA's federal budget. The Kennedy style that had led to a "swashbuckling" approach to taking the moon was anathema to the new president. Historian Alex Roland writes: "Nixon might publicly call the voyage of Apollo 11 'the greatest week in the history of the world since the Creation,' but he wasn't about to mortgage his administration and a distressed U.S. economy to a commitment that would look like an imitation of John Kennedy's famous man-on-the-moon proposal in 1961."[3]

So the interplanetary and interstellar focus at NASA shifted to smaller-budget unmanned scientific probes like the Viking and Voyager programs. These were messages in a bottle cast upon Kennedy's "vast new ocean" for someone to find while we on earth listened with parabolic ears.

Coming as it did in 1976, *Ratner's Star* is acutely aware of the unresolved social issues that preoccupied Bellow, Updike, Mailer, and Pynchon but chooses not to foreground them in quite the same way. Where those writers had been concerned with the huge gap between NASA's spectacles and the grittier social realities of America and the world, DeLillo seems to have already placed the moon shot as a diversionary spectacle of the previous decade. He is more interested in the scientific technocratic distillate of NASA's methods.

Field Experiment Number One follows the model of existing facilities such as the Theoretical Division at Los Alamos National Laboratory in New Mexico, the Jet Propulsion Laboratory in Pasadena, California, the Manned Spacecraft Center in Houston, Texas, and the Vehicle Assembly Building at Cape Canaveral, Florida. In all these places where abstract science is being engineered into form and substance, the hierarchical bureaucracy that has traditionally controlled the power/knowledge grid is dispersed horizontally among an ad hoc organization of specialists. Brought together in projects lasting only long enough to solve a specific multidisciplinary problem, the researchers are devoted to their individual disciplines and not to any governmental or corporate entity.

Researchers come and go at Field Experiment Number One. Even the shape of the structure housing the research resists any fixed architecture. The Cycloid, as it is called, is reminiscent of Mailer's description of the interior of the Vehicle Assembly Building at Cape Canaveral. Located on a "gray plain" in the desert, Field Experiment Number One is first revealed to Billy as a "sequined point . . . on the seam of land and air":

> Rising over the land and extending far across its breadth was a vast geometric structure, not at first recognizable as something designed to house or contain or harbor, simply a formulation, an expression in systematic terms of a fifty-story machine or educational toy or two-dimensional decorative object. The dominating shape seemed to be a cycloid, that elegant curve traced by a fixed point on the circumference of a circle rolling along a straight line, the line in this case being the land itself. . . . The cycloid was not complete, having no summit

or topmost arc, and . . . wedged inside the figure by a massive V-form steel support was the central element of the entire structure, a slowly rotating series of intersecting rings that suggested a medieval instrument of astronomy.

In all the structure was about sixteen hundred feet wide, six hundred feet high. Welded steel. Reinforced concrete. Translucent polyethylene. Aluminum, glass, mylar, sunstone. . . . Particular surfaces seemed to deflect light, causing perspectives to disappear and making it necessary to look away from time to time. Point line surface solid. Feeling of solar mirage. And still a building. A thing full of people. (15–16)

Ratner's Star, like the Cycloid, is a novel that foregrounds its structure. Daniel Aaron's observation that " 'plot' in his [DeLillo's] novels is the imposition of a design. Plots, like mathematics, make sense" is accurate, if you take in all the connotations of plot, especially those sinister, paranoid ones.[4] The Cycloid is unmappable. Every time Billy enters or exits a space within it, the configuration of doors and hallways appears different. At no time can he establish a set of coordinates that will allow him to know with any certainty where he is. His frame of reference is always shifting, as topologically distorted as the new physics being brought to bear on the communication from space.

It is useful to have more than a rudimentary familiarity with mathematics and particle physics to enjoy *Ratner's Star* fully. DeLillo himself calls the novel "a history of mathematics, a cult history, the names of the leaders kept secret until the second half of the book," because mathematics is the best example this world has of a nearly universal but nearly secret language "carried on almost totally outside the main currents of thought." [5]

Throughout the longer first section of the novel, "Adventures: Field Experiment Number One," the inexorable impulse of mathematical concepts to move out toward abstraction is used as a trope to examine the excessive abstraction of the efforts to decode the message from deep space. The best extended analysis of this is Tom LeClair's *In the Loop: Don DeLillo and the Systems Novel*. Though a bit too dogmatic in its effort to place DeLillo in a paradigm of Ludwig von Bertalanffy's *General Systems Theory,* it is nevertheless an intriguing and exhaustive study of how the formal structure of *Ratner's Star* depends on a linear history from the Mesopotamian concept of numbers to modern set theory.[6]

The shorter second section, "Reflections: Logicon Project Minus-One," which takes place below the dividing line of the earth's surface in the mirror-structure of the Cycloid, reverses that motion and traces a recursive arc from the far reaches of abstraction to the immediate and literal ground beneath Billy's feet. Following its major trope—"there is no reality more independent of our perception and more true to itself than mathematical reality"— the traditional novelistic concerns of character development and linear plot sequence are extraneous.[7] Billy Twillig even sees his own existence in terms of an equation, as a bicameral mind whose mathematical side "might overwhelm the other, leaving him behind, a name and shape" (129). Where Pynchon maps the contours of the Rocket state from the oneiric possibilities of Kekulé's work in chemistry, DeLillo informs Billy with a Cartesian terror of loneliness and faith in the ontology of numbers:

> From a series of three dreams had evolved a life fulfilled in mathematics and philosophy. The dreams had occurred within a single night. The first two concerned the terror of nature not understood and the last of them harbored a poem that pointed a way to the tasks of science. The world was comprehensible, a plane of equations, all knowledge able to be welded, all nature controllable. These were dreams generated by the motion of a straight line, a penciled breath of linear tension between day and night, the limit that separates numbers, positive from negative, real from imaginary, the dream-edge of discrete and continuous, history and prehistory, matter and

its mirror image. The dreamer, a soldier in repose, applied
the methods of algebra to the structure of geometry, bone-
setting the measured land, expressing his system in terms of
constants, variables and position coordinates, all arranged in
due time on the scheme of crossed lines forming squares of
equal size. (64)

This is, of course, the Newtonian view of the world that works
so well for engineers and created the technocratic culture of the
Space Age. For Bellow's Sammler, it plots the aerodynamic lift of
an aircraft's wing with no regard to the race, class, or gender of the
draftsman. For Updike's Angstrom, it creates the computer hardware to outmode everything in his life from the magnetic compass
to Verity Press. Likewise for Mailer, it is this logic that has created the leveling binomial nature of computers and now threatens
the last romantic stronghold of language itself. To Wolfe and to
Pynchon it is the structural model for a space program formed
reactively to handle the geopolitical flux of a Cold War missile
buildup. Out of the world redrawn at Potsdam emerged a technocratic model with a power grid as dispersed and convoluted
as a computer chip. The hierarchical ideal of authority had been
breached by lateral access.

Lateral or oblique access in *Ratner's Star* is part of the necessary tension of DeLillo's project. As the connotations and ety-
mology of Billy's name, "Twill" (OE *Twilic:* having a double thread),
suggests, things come in on the diagonal, warped into the dense
fabric of ideas. Everything, from the exact knowledge of who is
directing the project, to the fixed spatiality of the Cycloid structure, and even the very objective of the project itself, is unavailable
to specific, concrete location. But there is always a sense of con-
vergence. What is available to all is information, vast abstract data
that can be arranged and rearranged to address any number of
problems. The explanation U. F. O. Schwarz offers to Billy Twillig
concerning the radio transmissions from space is representative:

We picked them up on the synthesis telescope. They transmitted and we received. Pulses. Signals were transmitted in
irregular pulses. We happened to be tuned to the right frequency. Space Brain [a supercomputer] has printed out a tape
covered with zeros and ones. Mostly ones. . . . One hundred
and one pulses and gaps. The pulses we interpret as ones. The
gaps or pauses as zeros. . . .

Space Brain has printed out hundreds of interpretations
without coming up with anything we can call definitive.
Dozens of men and women have also failed. Radio astrono-
mers, chemists, exobiologists, mathematicians, physicists,
cryptanalysts, paleographers, linguists, computer linguists,
cosmic linguists. (47)

Definitive is the operative word here. The inability to fix the
limits, and thereby stabilize the meaning of the binomial transmission that has come in on the frequency to which the researchers
"happened" to be tuned, represents a failure of technocratic policy
over scientific method. Schwarz tells Billy: "What we need at this
stage of our perceptual development is an overarching symmetry.
Something that constitutes what it appears to be—even if it isn't—
a totally harmonious picture of the world system" (49).

DeLillo introduces an amazing array of characters devoted
to creating closed systems that will encompass the abstract and
the uncertain. From Billy's Bronx childhood DeLillo offers parents
whose lives are saturated with the mass values of television and
twentieth-century urban existence. Babe and Faye believe in the
one-to-one correspondence of words to things. For them expression
is possible. Babe believes Faye can describe his batting stance accu-
rately enough over the telephone for one of his buddies to guess
who he is imitating. Faye believes in the communicative force of
dramatic presence: "Settled in front of the TV set with a lapful of
muscatel grapes, Faye pointed out to Billy why certain performers
were considered classic" (73).

The "scream lady," who lives in an apartment across the air shaft, constructs a paranoid totality in twisted idiom, syntax, and numerology. Though none of the words she shrieks seems "to belong to any known language," the handwritten message she gives to Billy has its own discrete logic:

Stock mark ave/rage (549.74 929/1929) grim pill
of pilgrim welfare (fare/well) scumsuckers inc.
& brownshirt king/pres. (press/king) of U.S. of
S/hit/ler & secret (seek/credit) dung of U.S.
Cong/Viet Cong & Christ/of/fear Columbus discovered
syph / ill / U.S. 1492+1929=3421 / 1234 / 4321 astro / bones
buried
under ever/grin tree in Rock/fooler Center 50+
5 Ave.=55 St/Ave/Stave (Cane Abe/L/incoln 1865+
1492+1929 = 5286/PANCA DVI ASTA SAS (73)

The "scream lady's" obsession with sequence appears to be the sort of numerological paranoia, or "cryptic numeroglyphics" (249), that drives less deranged (or perhaps *more* deranged) cranks to neoconservative conspiracy theories. But in *Ratner's Star,* she functions as part of the degraded urban landscape that an Artur Sammler or Harry Angstrom, riding their buses through the cities of America, might see without noticing.

DeLillo's use of paranoia is a bit more playful than Pynchon's but no less pervasive. Another character, Cheops Feely, has developed a microelectronic implant that does much the same thing as the oneirine theophosphate in *Gravity's Rainbow.* Feely and his research associate have developed "a device that would greatly simplify manned space missions . . . increase an astronaut's capabilities a thousandfold" (242). The "Leduc Electrode," as it is called, would mate a tiny computer to the brain by way of surgical implant, but it has one drawback: "The problem with the device as now constituted is that it tends to overstimulate the left side of the brain. This will result in an overpowering sense of sequence. You'll be acutely aware of the arrangement of things. The order of succession of events. The way one thing leads to another. . . . You'll be involved in a very detailed treatment of reality. A parody of the left brain. But is that reality of yours less valid than ordinary reality? Not at all" (245).

There is also Endor, another of the world's greatest mathematicians, who has fled from the project and now lives in a hole eating insect larvae rather than deal with the implications of what his efforts to decode the message from space might mean.

Then there is Chester Greylag Dent, "The Supreme Abstract Commander," who rides not above it all but below it—thirty-five thousand feet beneath the ocean. Chester Greylag Dent, another surname redolent with images of a surface deformed but not broken by pressure, its sides converging toward that point of maximum force. A parody of Jules Verne's Captain Nemo—who fled the earth's surface to wreak his own anarchistic havoc on the warships of the world—Dent is, as Frank Lentricchia calls him, DeLillo's "funny anecdotal personification . . . of a fear not really separable from the modernist dream," the horror of abstraction actively engaged in reinscribing even the private particularities of small things.[8]

Other players in the technocratic stakes are Edna Lown, Lester Bolin, and Maurice Wu, researchers engaged in developing a "universal" language based on rigorous mathematical principles, which would enable them to communicate with extraterrestrials. The second section of the novel, "Reflections: Logicon Project Minus-One," shifts the action away from Billy's efforts to solve the radio transmission to his work with Wu and Bolin on the universal language. It is a shift in physical space as well. Whereas the outer-directed research on decoding the message was located within the raised curve of the Cycloid's arching structure, the language project is being carried out in the subterranean mirror image of the Cycloid.

DeLillo creates wonderful scenes for all these characters to present their beliefs, but the one who gets the most play is Elux

Troxl, the head of an international cartel with "an undrinkable greed for the abstract," who is engaged in acquiring "air space" and commodifying time—computer, makeshift, standby, conceptual—in order to regulate the international "money curve" (146–47). Troxl and his cartel named ACRONYM, "a combination of letters formed to represent the idea of a combination of letters" (344), are the latest mutation of multinational capitalism. Far beyond the manufacturing intrigues of IG Farben and Dutch Shell, Troxl's operation deals strictly in information (mailing lists, subscription research, and the like) and the rental of computer time.

Troxl moves throughout much of *Ratner's Star* on the periphery of actual control of Field Experiment Number One and its supercomputer. By the end of the novel, ACRONYM has acquired all the "model-building organizations," including Field Experiment Number One, the Logicon Project Minus-One, and the Center for the Refinement of Ideational Structures, and appears to have succeeded in creating a globally closed system. But the world is in turmoil, all the conventional lines of communication in disarray: "International tensions. Mounting international tensions. First there were states of precautionary alert. Then there were enhanced readiness contours. This was followed by maximum arc situation preparedness. We can measure the gravity of events by tracing the increasingly abstract nature of the terminology. One more level of vagueness and that could be it. . . . We're dealing with global euphemisms now" (281).

Ratner's Star is linked to *Gravity's Rainbow* not merely by its encyclopedic aspirations, its deployment of recent theoretical and mathematical concepts, and its satirical wit, but also in the way both works question the wisdom of placing the world's fate solely in the hands of scientists and technocrats. Where the other narratives are troubled by technology but still "believe" in it (yes, even Mailer) in the sense that they never really question the linear progression of up, out, and away, DeLillo and Pynchon continually offer up alternate cosmologies from an earlier, more ceremonial, view of "the order of things." Bellow, Updike, Mailer, and Wolfe might question priorities and the expense and timing of large-scale projects like Apollo, but none of them really seems to question the underlying faith in technique.

DeLillo, on the other hand, has taken a satiric look at what happens when a surfeit of technique is brought to bear on a paucity of data. The number of specialists brought in to work on decoding the message from space seems to reach critical mass after the symposium in the Great Hole (misheard as "Great Hall" by Billy), and the densely compressed intellectual energy explodes into a multitude of new projects, among them the Logicon Project Minus-One.

In a way, the reorientation of Billy's mission is a little like Wolfe's narrative of Project Mercury, when the crisis caused by *Sputnik* drove American policymakers virtually to scrap the very successful X-series rocket program and start anew with ballistic rockets. Though the X-series limped along with minimal funding and provided much of the technology that has made the Space Shuttle what it is—a dangerous high-tech, low-budget compromise—the research was much delayed and only incompletely realized.

Billy's eventual decoding of the message is equally delayed and even more useless. Following Maurice Wu's lead that archaeological evidence might support a longer curve and a more catastrophic periodicity to human civilization, Billy discovers that the message is in fact a terrestrial warning based on ancient Mesopotamian notation by sixty. The message had been sent into space by some ancient civilization whose scientific sophistication was sufficient to understand the concept of "curved space." It warns of an unscheduled eclipse, or a "noncognate celestial anomaly," as one of DeLillo's characters refers to it in the language of abstract scientific bureaucracy.

DeLillo's description of the terror inspired by this unexpected but ultimately benign event is marvelously parodic of apocalyptic narratives. It is a sobering social commentary as well because the moon's shadow, as it races in a northeast arc across the rotating surface of the earth, darkens first the East:

> The eclipse path and its outer borders of partial darkness re-
> sembles a charred immensity, children with begging bowls,
> men surrendered to meditation. . . . Children immobilized by
> gastroenteritis, scavenging to live, to know what passes above,
> this nearly sunset occurrence, shadow moving toward the east-
> most Ganges, choleroid feces, choleroid dehydration. . . . It is
> as everywhere, the soul of one experience passing untouched
> through the soul of another. . . . Having dismantled the handi-
> work of your own perceptions in order to solve reality, you
> know it now as a micron flash of light-scattering matter in a
> structure otherwise composed of purely mathematical coordi-
> nates. (430–31)

The solid four-page paragraph traces the sweep of the eclipse, as DeLillo alternates a description of the abstract and the concrete, of Eastern mystic renunciation of earthly concerns and the abject poverty that weighs so heavily on the land. It is a region as removed from the sterility of Field Experiment Number One as is ideologi- cally possible yet no less prepared for what is happening than the researchers themselves. In the face of an event unforeseen by mod- ern scientific rationalism, ritual magic has as much to offer: "Inside our desolation, however, you come upon the reinforcing grid of works and minds that extend themselves against whatever lonely spaces account for our hollow moods, the woe incoming" (432).

As readers we are viewing it all from Hannah Arendt's Archi- medean point in space, a point no longer dependent on powers of imagination and abstraction to envision but now made familiar by the cameras of Apollo missions. We have seen the blue earth shin- ing out from the void, and it is now possible to imagine the racing shadow that cuts across it.

So it is the anomalous event, the failure of celestial mechanics to adhere to Newtonian calculus, even though theoretical physics had discarded any reason why it should, that reopens a space in DeLillo's fictive world for mystery. Similar to the temporary grid available to the counterforce in the "Zone" of Pynchon's fiction, this reanimation of mystery in a world given over to rationalism is not intended as a cosmology outside the technocratic grid, but rather within it, at "the contact line of nature and mathematical thought . . . where things make sense, things accede to our view of them, things return to us a propagating wave of reason" (431).

Unlike Mailer, who fears that science will overwhelm nature, or Pynchon, who fears that it might be obliterated, DeLillo seems to find some hope in our newfound ability to see the earth whole. Our technology has followed a parabolic curve that, in the mid-1970s, seems to be arcing back toward a more fundamental understanding of the fragile biosystem that supports us all. It isn't as absurd as it first seems that the bible of every early 1970s back-to-the-land commune, *The Whole Earth Catalogue,* featured on its cover the classic photograph of earth shot by *Apollo 8*. Orbiting out beyond the earth's incomplete curvature, out where it is possible to view desert regions and teeming cities simultaneously, where it is possible to know the aboriginal world as well as the technocratic, it isn't possible to believe so discretely in science. Things have a way of bending back on themselves just as the recursive flow of *Ratner's Star* does.

Notes

1. Fire and Power: A Narrative of the Space Age

1 *Facts Book: Eastern Space and Missile Center,* ed. Public Affairs Office, Patrick Air Force Base, Fla., 1982, 71.

2 Henry Adams, *The Education of Henry Adams,* ed. Ernest Samuels (Boston: Houghton Mifflin, 1973), 379–90.

3 Walter McDougall, . . . *the Heavens and the Earth: A Political History of the Space Age* (New York: Basic Books, 1985), 317.

4 In addition to McDougall's . . . *the Heavens and the Earth,* see William H. Chafe, *The Unfinished Journey: America Since World War II* (New York: Oxford University Press, 1986), and Dale Carter, *The Final Frontier: The Rise and Fall of the American Rocket State* (London: Verso, 1988), for accounts of the global expansion of U.S. technical and economic interests.

5 Michael L. Smith, "Selling the Moon: The U.S. Manned Space Program and the Triumph of Commodity Scientism," in *The Culture of Consumption: Critical Essays in American History, 1880–1980,* ed. Richard Wrightman Fox and T. J. Jackson Lears (New York: Pantheon Books, 1983), 175–209.

6 Norman Mailer, *Of a Fire on the Moon* (Boston: Little, Brown, 1970), 43.

7 McDougall, . . . *the Heavens and the Earth,* v.

8 Mailer, *Of a Fire on the Moon,* 129.

9 Fredric Jameson, "Periodizing the Sixties," in *The Ideologies of Theory: Essays, 1971–1986* (Minneapolis: University of Minnesota Press, 1988), 200.

10 Among the best works concerned with the impact of the space program on American literature are Ronald Weber's *Seeing Earth: Literary Responses to Space Exploration* (Athens: Ohio University Press, 1985); Laurence Goldstein's *The Flying Machine and Modern Literature* (Bloomington: Indiana University

Press, 1986); and George Held's "Men on the Moon: American Novelists Explore Lunar Space," which, along with early chapters of Weber's, Goldstein's, and Walter McDougall's works, appeared in a special issue of the *Michigan Quarterly Review* 18 (Spring 1979) commemorating the tenth anniversary of the first lunar landing. Besides McDougall's fine work, see Carter's *Final Frontier.* H. Bruce Franklin's *War Stars: The Superweapon and the American Imagination* (New York: Oxford University Press, 1988) offers an interesting cultural critique that often depends on literary texts.

11   Fredric Jameson, "Postmodernism, or The Cultural Logic of Late Capitalism," *New Left Review,* no. 146 (July–August 1984): 83–84.

12   Ibid., 54–56.

13   Collette Brooks, "Notes on American Mythology," *Partisan Review* 15 (1988): 314.

14   Saul Bellow, *Mr. Sammler's Planet* (New York: Viking Press, 1970); John Updike, *Rabbit Redux* (New York: Knopf, 1971); Mailer, *Of a Fire on the Moon;* Tom Wolfe, *The Right Stuff* (New York: Farrar, Straus, and Giroux, 1979); Thomas Pynchon, *Gravity's Rainbow* (New York: Viking Press, 1973); Don DeLillo, *Ratner's Star* (New York: Knopf, 1976).

15   Norman Mailer, Thomas Pynchon, and Walter McDougall all incorporate Von Braun's statement to the effect that the moon landing would be the greatest event in history since aquatic life had moved up onto land.

16   John Dos Passos, *Century's Ebb: The Thirteenth Chronicle* (Boston: Gambit, 1975), 467.

17   Norman Mailer, *Cannibals and Christians* (New York: Dial Press, 1965), 95–96.

18   Oriana Fallaci, "Norman Mailer: Why Do People Dislike America?" in Fallaci, *The Egotists: Sixteen Surprising Interviews* (Chicago: Henry Regenery, 1968), 6–7.

19   Michel Foucault, *Power/Knowledge: Selected Interviews and Other Writings, 1972–1977,* ed. Colin Gordon, trans. Colin Gordon, Leo Marshall, John Mepham, and Kate Soper (New York: Pantheon Books, 1980), 98.

20   Vincent B. Leitch, *American Literary Criticism from the Thirties to the Eighties* (New York: Columbia University Press, 1988), 150. The texts Leitch lists are David Riesman's *Lonely Crowd* (1950), C. Wright Mills's *White Collar* (1951) and *The Power Elite* (1956), Herbert Marcuse's *Eros and Civilization* (1955), William Whyte's *Organization Man* (1956), Vance Packard's *Hidden Persuaders* (1957), John Kenneth Galbraith's *Affluent Society* (1958), Norman O. Brown's *Life Against Death* (1959), and Paul Goodman's *Growing Up Absurd* (1960).

21   Mailer, *Of a Fire on the Moon,* 12.

22   Ibid., 54.

2. *Machines for Going Away: Mr. Sammler*
and the Labor of Puritanism

1   Stanley Fish, *Surprised by Sin: The Reader in "Paradise Lost"* (Berkeley and Los
    Angeles: University of California Press, 1971), 220n.

2   Bellow, *Mr. Sammler's Planet,* 32. Subsequent citations are in parentheses in
    the text.

3   Earl Rovit, "Saul Bellow and Norman Mailer: The Secret Sharers," in *Saul Bel-
    low: A Collection of Essays,* ed. Rovit (Englewood Cliffs, N.J.: Prentice-Hall,
    1975), 163.

4   Benjamin DeMott, "Saul Bellow and the Dogmas of Possibility," *Saturday Re-
    view,* February 7, 1970, pp. 25–28, 37.

5   Robert R. Dutton, *Saul Bellow* (New York: Twayne, 1971), 11.

6   Donald H. Menzel, "Space—The New Frontier," *PMLA* 77 (1962): 10–17;
    Hannah Arendt, "Man's Conquest of Space," *American Scholar* 32 (Autumn
    1963): 527–40.

7   Beverly Gross, "Dark Side of the Moon," *Nation* 210 (February 8, 1970): 154;
    James Neal Harris, "One Critical Approach to *Mr. Sammler's Planet,*" *Twentieth
    Century Literature* 18 (October 1972): 235–70; D. P. M. Salter, "Optimism and
    Reaction in Saul Bellow's Recent Work," *Critical Quarterly* 14 (Spring 1972): 64.

8   Full translations of Weber's work were just becoming available around the time
    Bellow was writing *Mr. Sammler's Planet.* A three-volume edition of *Economy
    and Society: An Outline of Interpretive Sociology* was published in 1969 by Bed-
    minster Press. *On Charisma and Institution Building; Selected Papers* was also
    published in 1969 by the University of Chicago Press. For another popular
    writer equally quick to employ Weber, see Alvin Toffler, *Future Shock* (New
    York: Random House, 1970), 128.

9   Arendt, "Man's Conquest of Space," 540.

10 Rovit, "Saul Bellow and Norman Mailer," 161–70.

11 Gordon Lloyd Harper, "Saul Bellow," in *Writers at Work: The Paris Review
    Interviews, Third Series,* ed. George Plimpton (New York: Viking Press, 1968),
    189–90.

3. *Docile Bodies at Verity Press:*
Disciplinary Space in Rabbit Redux

1   Updike, *Rabbit Redux,* 27. Subsequent citations are in parentheses in the text.

2   Robert Merton, forword to Jacques Ellul, *The Technological Society,* trans. John
    Wilkinson (New York: Vintage, 1964), v.

3   Dilvo I. Ristoff, *Updike's America: The Presence of Contemporary American History in John Updike's Rabbit Trilogy* (New York: Peter Lang, 1988), 101.

4. Between a Rock and a Hard Face: Norman Mailer's
Of a Fire on the Moon

1   Quoted in Mailer, *Of a Fire on the Moon,* 5. Subsequent citations are in parentheses in the text.

2   Wolfe, *Right Stuff,* 45, 46.

3   Richard Poirier, "The Ups and Downs of Mailer," *New Republic,* January 23, 1971, p. 23.

4   Philip Bufithis, "Norman Mailer," *Dictionary of Literary Biography,* vol. 2 (Detroit: Gale Research, 1978), 279–80; Peter Manso, *Mailer: His Life and Times* (New York: Simon and Schuster, 1985), 34–37.

5   Norman Mailer, *The Naked and the Dead* (New York: Holt, Rinehart, and Winston, 1948), 443–44.

6   Richard Poirier, *Norman Mailer* (New York: Viking Press, 1972), 25.

7   Gordon O. Taylor, "Of Adams and Aquarius," *American Literature* 46 (1974): 69.

8   Ibid., 72.

9   Leo Marx, "The Impact of the Railroad on the American Imagination, as a Possible Comparison for the Space Impact," and Bruce Mazlish, "Historical Analogy: The Railroad and the Space Program and Their Impact on Society," in *The Railroad and the Space Program: An Exploration in Historical Analogy,* ed. Mazlish (Cambridge, Mass.: MIT Press, 1965).

10 Toffler, *Future Shock,* 112–35.

11 Michel Foucault, *Discipline and Punish: The Birth of the Prison,* trans. from the French by Alan Sheridan (New York: Vintage, 1979), 154.

12 Goldstein, *The Flying Machine in American Literature,* 203.

13 Chris Anderson, *Style as Argument: Contemporary American Nonfiction* (Carbondale: Southern Illinois University Press, 1987), 90.

5. Desert Space and the High Frontier:
Tom Wolfe as Text Pilot

1   Mailer, *Of a Fire on the Moon,* 52.

2   Michael Collins, *Carrying the Fire: An Astronaut's Journey* (New York: Farrar, Straus, and Giroux, 1974), 4.

3   Wolfe, *Right Stuff,* 48. Subsequent citations are in parentheses in the text.

4   Edward T. Hall, *The Hidden Dimension* (Garden City, N.Y.: Doubleday, 1966),

26–32, 166–68. (Tom Wolfe profiled Edward T. Hall and his work in a chapter, "O Rotten Gotham—Sliding Down into the Behavioral Sink," in *The Pump House Gang* [New York: Farrar, Straus, and Giroux, 1968], 231–44.)

5   Tom Wolfe, "Post-Orbital Remorse: How the Astronauts Fell from Cowboy Heaven," *Rolling Stone*, no. 128 (January 18, 1973): 23.

6   Ibid.

7   Wolfe, *Right Stuff*, 53–59.

8   John H. Glenn, "Glitches in Time Save Trouble," in M. Scott Carpenter, L. Gordon Cooper, John H. Glenn, Jr., et al., *We Seven* (New York: Simon and Schuster, 1962), 216.

9   Chris Anderson, *Argument as Style: Contemporary American Nonfiction* (Carbondale: Southern Illinois University Press, 1987), 13.

10 Mailer, *Of a Fire on the Moon*, 34.

11 Yeager's public image as a no-nonsense man with "the right stuff" was so pervasive in the 1980s that he was appointed to the civilian review board of the Space Shuttle *Challenger* disaster even though he had never had any direct involvement with the Space Transportation System program. He was apparently part of a public relations gambit by NASA that did not pay off, and he eventually resigned from the commission after complaints were made public by others on the board about his continual absence from key meetings.

6. Chemistry and Colonialism Gone Ballistic:
Apprehending the Mass of Gravity's Rainbow

1   Pynchon, *Gravity's Rainbow*, 737–38. Subsequent citations are in parentheses in the text.

2   Mathew Winston, "The Quest for Thomas Pynchon," *Mindful Pleasures: Essays on Thomas Pynchon*, in ed. George Levine and David Leverenz (Boston: Little, Brown, 1976), 260.

3   *The Compact Edition of the Oxford English Dictionary* (New York: Oxford University Press, 1971), 3212.

4   Steven Weisenburger, *A Gravity's Rainbow Companion: Sources and Contexts for Pynchon's Novel* (Athens: University of Georgia Press, 1988), 1.

5   See Scott Sanders, "Pynchon's Paranoid History," *Twentieth Century Literature* 21 (May 1975): 177–92; Lawrence Wofley, "Repression's Rainbow: The Presence of Norman O. Brown in Pynchon's Big Novel," *PMLA* 92 (1977): 873–89; Thomas S. Smith, "Performing in the Zone: The Presentation of Historical Crisis in *Gravity's Rainbow*," *CLIO* 12 (Spring 1983): 245–60; Raymond Mazurek, "Ideology and Form in the Postmodernist Novel: *The Sot-Weed Factor* and

Gravity's Rainbow," *Minnesota Review* n.s., 25 (1985): 69–84; Brian Stonehill, *The Self-Conscious Novel: Artifice in Fiction from Joyce to Pynchon* (Philadelphia: University of Pennsylvania Press, 1988); Carter, *Final Frontier.*

6   Georg Lukács, *The Historical Novel,* trans. Hannah Mitchell and Stanley Mitchell (1963; rpt. Lincoln: University of Nebraska Press, 1983), 337–38.

7   Mazurek, "Ideology and Form," 77.

8   Stonehill, *Self-Conscious Novel,* 142.

9   Sanders, "Pynchon's Paranoid History," 183.

10   Edward Mendelson, "Gravity's Encyclopedia," in *Mindful Pleasures: Essays on Thomas Pynchon* (Boston: Little, Brown, 1976), 168.

11   Max Weber, *The Theory of Social and Economic Organization,* trans. Talcott Parsons and A. M. Henderson (New York: Oxford University Press, 1947), 364.

12   James E. Webb quoted in McDougall, . . . *the Heavens and the Earth,* 388.

13   Weisenburger, Gravity's Rainbow *Companion,* 94.

14   Ibid., 237.

15   Ibid., 238.

16   Norman Mailer, *Why Are We in Vietnam?* (New York: Putnam, 1967), 85.

17   Michael Herr, *Dispatches* (New York: Avon Books, 1977), 51.

7. *Terror in a Lonely Place: Anomie and Anomaly in* Ratner's Star

1   Carter, *Final Frontier,* 204–5. According to Carter, the space program created more than twenty thousand jobs directly and another thirty thousand indirectly in Brevard County between 1961 and 1966.

2   DeLillo, *Ratner's Star,* 4. Subsequent citations are given in parentheses in the text.

3   Alex Roland, "The Shuttle: Triumph or Turkey," *Discover* 6 (November 1985): 30–31.

4   Daniel Aaron, "How to Read Don DeLillo," *South Atlantic Quarterly* 89 (Spring 1990): 316.

5   Tom LeClair, "An Interview with Don DeLillo," in *Anything Can Happen: Interviews with Contemporary American Novelists,* ed. Tom LeClair and Larry McCaffrey (Urbana: University of Illinois Press, 1983), 86.

6   Tom LeClair, *In the Loop: Don DeLillo and the Systems Novel* (Urbana: University of Illinois Press, 1987), 111–44.

7   DeLillo, *Ratner's Star,* 48.

8   Frank Lentricchia, *Ariel and the Police: Michel Foucault, William James, Wallace Stevens* (Madison: University of Wisconsin Press, 1988), 23–24.

Bibliography

Adams, Hazard. *Philosophy of the Literary Symbolic.* Tallahassee: University Presses of Florida, 1983.

Adams, Henry. *The Education of Henry Adams.* Edited by Ernest Samuels. Boston: Houghton Mifflin, 1973.

Arendt, Hannah. *The Human Condition.* Chicago: University of Chicago Press, 1958.

———. "Man's Conquest of Space." *American Scholar* 32 (Autumn 1963): 527–40.

Armstrong, Neil, with Gene Farmer and Dora Jean Hamblin. *First on the Moon: A Voyage with Neil Armstrong, Michael Collins, Edwin E. Aldrin, Jr.* Boston: Little, Brown, 1970.

Aronowitz, Stanley. *Science as Power: Discourse and Ideology in Modern Society.* Minneapolis: University of Minnesota Press, 1988.

Barrett, William. *The Illusion of Technique.* New York: Anchor Books/Doubleday, 1978.

———. *Time of Need: Forms of Imagination in the Twentieth Century.* New York: Harper & Row, 1972.

Barthes, Roland. "The Jet-Man." In *Mythologies.* New York: Hill and Wang, 1972.

Bauer, Raymond. *Second-Order Consequences: A Methodological Essay on the Impact of Technology.* Cambridge, Mass.: MIT Press, 1969.

Bellow, Saul. *Mr. Sammler's Planet.* New York: Viking Press, 1970.

Bilstein, Roger. *Flight in America, 1900–1983: From the Wrights to the Astronauts.* Baltimore: Johns Hopkins University Press, 1984.

Bochner, Salomon. *The Role of Mathematics in the Rise of Science.* Princeton: Princeton University Press, 1966.

Boorstin, Daniel. *Democracy and Its Discontents: Reflections on Everyday America.* New York: Random House, 1974.

Boyer, Paul. *By the Bomb's Early Light: American Thought and Culture at the Dawn of the Atomic Age.* New York: Pantheon, 1985.

Carter, Dale. *The Final Frontier: The Rise and Fall of the American Rocket State.* London: Verso, 1988.

Carter, Paul. "Rockets to the Moon, 1919–1944: A Dialogue Between Fiction and Reality." *American Studies* 15 (1974): 31–46.

Cassirer, Ernst. *The Individual and the Cosmos in Renaissance Philosophy.* 1927. Reprint. New York: Harper Torchbooks, 1964.

Chafe, William H. *The Unfinished Journey: America Since World War II.* New York: Oxford University Press, 1986.

Collins, Michael. *Carrying the Fire: An Astronaut's Journey.* New York: Farrar, Straus, and Giroux, 1974.

Corn, Joseph J. *Imagining Tomorrow: History, Technology, and the American Future.* Cambridge, Mass.: MIT Press, 1986.

————. *The Winged Gospel: America' Romance with Aviation, 1900–1950.* New York: Oxford University Press, 1983.

DeLillo, Don. "Human Moments in World War III." *Esquire,* July 1983, pp. 118–26.

————. *Ratner's Star.* 1976. Reprint. New York: Vintage Books, 1980.

————. *White Noise.* New York: Viking Press, 1985.

DeMott, Benjamin. "Saul Bellow and the Dogmas of Possibility." *Saturday Review,* February 7, 1970, pp. 25–28, 37.

Dickey, James. *The Eye Beaters, Blood, Victory, Madness, Buckhead and Mercy.* Garden City, N.Y.: Doubleday, 1970.

Dos Passos, John. *Century's Ebb: The Thirteenth Chronicle.* Boston: Gambit, 1975.

————. "On the Way to the Moon Shot." *National Review,* February 9, 1971, pp. 135–36.

Dutton, Robert R. *Saul Bellow.* New York: Twayne, 1971.

Dyson, Freeman. *Disturbing the Universe.* New York: Harper & Row, 1979.

Etzioni, Amitai. *The Moon-Doggle.* Garden City, N.Y.: Doubleday, 1964.

Fallaci, Oriani. *If the Sun Dies.* Translated by Pamela Swinglehurst. New York: Atheneum, 1968.

————. "Norman Mailer: Why Do People Dislike America?" In *The Egotists: Sixteen Surprising Interviews.* Chicago: Henry Regnery, 1968.

Ferkiss, Victor C. *Technological Man: The Myth and the Reality.* New York: George Braziller, 1969.

Fish, Stanley. *Surprised by Sin: The Reader in "Paradise Lost."* Berkeley and Los Angeles: University of California Press, 1971.

Foucault, Michel. *Discipline and Punish: The Birth of the Prison.* New York: Vintage, 1979.

————. *The Order of Things: An Archaeology of the Human Sciences.* New York: Random House, 1970.

————. *Power/Knowledge: Selected Interviews and Other Writings, 1972–1977.* Edited by Colin Gordon. Translated by Colin Gordon, Leo Marshall, John Mepham, and Kate Soper. Brighton: Havester Press, 1980.

Franklin, H. Bruce. *War Stars: The Superweapon and the American Imagination.* New York: Oxford University Press, 1988.

Friedman, Alan J. "Contemporary American Physics Fiction." *American Journal of Physics* 47 (1979): 392–95.

Gleick, James. *Chaos: Making a New Science.* New York: Penguin, 1987.

Goldstein, Laurence. *The Flying Machine in Modern Literature.* Bloomington: Indiana University Press, 1986.

————. "The Moon Landing and Its Aftermath." *Michigan Quarterly Review* 18 (Spring 1979): 318–42.

Greiner, Donald J. *John Updike's Novels.* Athens: Ohio University Press, 1984.

Gross, Beverly. "Dark Side of the Moon." *Nation* 210 (February 8, 1970): 154.

Harper, Gordon Lloyd. "Saul Bellow." In *Writers at Work: The Paris Review Interviews, Third Series,* edited by George Plimpton, 189–90. New York: Viking Press, 1968.

Harris, James Neal. "One Critical Approach to *Mr. Sammler's Planet.*" *Twentieth Century Literature* 18 (October 1972): 235–70.

Harvey, David. *The Condition of Postmodernity: An Enquiry into the Origins of Cultural Change.* Oxford: Basil Blackwell, 1989.

Hassan, Ihab. *The Right Promethean Fire: Imagination, Science, and Cultural Change.* Urbana: University of Illinois Press, 1980.

Held, George. "Men on the Moon: American Novelists Explore Lunar Space." *Michigan Quarterly Review* 18 (Spring 1979): 318–42.

Hilleges, Mark R. *The Future as Nightmare: H. G. Wells and the Anti-Utopians.* New York: Oxford University Press, 1967.

Holmes, Jay. *America on the Moon: The Enterprise of the Sixties.* Philadelphia: J. B. Lippincott, 1962.

Hutcheon, Linda. *A Poetics of Postmodernism: History, Theory, Fiction.* New York: Routledge, 1988.

Jameson, Fredric. *The Political Unconscious: Narrative as a Socially Symbolic Act.* Ithaca: Cornell University Press, 1981.

————. "Postmodernism, or, the Cultural Logic of Late Capitalism." *New Left Review* 146 (September 1984): 53–92.

Kernan, Alvin B. *The Imaginary Library: An Essay on Literature and Society.* Princeton: Princeton University Press, 1982.

Kuhn, Thomas S. *The Essential Tension: Selected Studies in Scientific Tradition and Change.* Chicago: University of Chicago Press, 1977.

Lavery, David. *Late for the Sky: The Mentality of the Space Age.* Carbondale: Southern Illinois University Press, 1992.

LeClair, Tom. "An Interview with Don DeLillo." In *Anything Can Happen: Interviews with Contemporary American Authors,* edited by Tom LeClair and Larry McCaffrey, 79–90. Urbana: University of Illinois Press, 1983.

———. *In the Loop: Don DeLillo and the Systems Novel.* Urbana: University of Illinois Press, 1987.

Leitch, Vincent B. *American Literary Criticism from the Thirties to the Eighties.* New York: Columbia University Press, 1988.

Lentricchia, Frank. "The American Writer as Bad Citizen—Introducing Don DeLillo." *South Atlantic Quarterly* 89 (Spring 1990): 239–44.

———. *Ariel and the Police: Michel Foucault, William James, Wallace Stevens.* Madison: University of Wisconsin Press, 1988.

Lodge, David. *The Modes of Modern Writing: Metaphor, Metonymy, and the Typology of Modern Literature.* Chicago: University of Chicago Press, 1988.

Mailer, Norman. *Of a Fire on the Moon.* Boston: Little, Brown, 1970.

———. *Why Are We in Vietnam?* New York: Putnam, 1967.

Manso, Peter. *Mailer: His Life and Times.* New York: Simon and Schuster, 1985.

Marx, Leo. "American Literary Culture and the Fatalistic View of Technology." In *The Pilot and the Passenger: Essays on Literature, Technology, and Culture in the United States.* New York: Oxford University Press, 1988.

———. *The Machine in the Garden: Technology and the Pastoral Idea in America.* New York: Oxford University Press, 1964.

———. "Reflections on the Neo-Romantic Critique of Science." *Daedalus* 107 (1978): 61–74.

Mazlish, Bruce, ed. *The Railroad and the Space Program: An Exploration in Historical Analogy.* Cambridge, Mass.: MIT Press, 1965.

McDougall, Walter A. "Technology and Statecraft in the Space Age—Toward a History of Salvation." *American Historical Review* 87 (October 1982): 1010–40.

———. *. . . the Heavens and the Earth: A Political History of the Space Age.* New York: Basic Books, 1985.

McFarland, Marvin W., ed. *The Papers of Wilbur and Orville Wright.* New York: McGraw-Hill, 1953.

McHale, Brian. *Constructing Postmodernism.* London: Routledge, 1992.

———. *Postmodernist Fiction.* New York: Methuen, 1987.

McLuhan, Marshall. *The Mechanical Bride: Folklore of Industrial Man.* New York: Vanguard Press, 1951.

Menzel, Donald H. "Space—The New Frontier." *PMLA* 77 (1962): 10–17.

Michener, James A. *Space*. New York: Random House, 1982.

Nadeau, Robert. *Readings from the New Book on Nature: Physics and Metaphysics in the Modern Novel*. Amherst: University of Massachusetts Press, 1981.

Phillips, Jayne Ann. *Machine Dreams*. New York: Dutton/Lawrence, 1984.

Pynchon, Thomas. *Gravity's Rainbow*. New York: Viking Press, 1973.

Rhodes, Richard. *Sons of Earth*. New York: Coward, McCann & Geohegan, 1981.

Ristoff, Dilvo I. *Updike's America: The Presence of Contemporary American History in John Updike's Rabbit Trilogy*. New York: Peter Lang, 1988.

Rovit, Earl. "Saul Bellow and Norman Mailer: The Secret Sharers." In *Saul Bellow: A Collection of Essays,* edited by Earl Rovit. Englewood Cliffs, N.J.: Prentice-Hall, 1975.

Salter, D. P. M. "Optimism and Reaction in Saul Bellow's Recent Work." *Critical Quarterly* 14 (Spring 1972): 64.

Sanders, Scott. "The Left-Handedness of Modern Literature." *Twentieth Century Literature* 23 (1977): 417–36.

Stark, John O. *Pynchon's Fictions: Thomas Pynchon and the Literature of Information*. Athens: Ohio University Press, 1980.

Stupple, James. "A Literature Against the Future." *American Scholar* (Spring 1977): 215–20.

Sypher, Wylie. *Literature and Technology: The Alien Vision*. New York: Random House, 1968.

Toffler, Alvin. *Future Shock*. New York: Random House, 1970.

Updike, John. "The Moons of Jupiter." *American Scholar* (Autumn 1982): 484–86.

———. *Rabbit Redux*. New York: Knopf, 1971.

Van Dyke, Vernon. *Pride and Power: The Rationale of the Space Program*. Urbana: University of Illinois Press, 1964.

Von Braun, Wernher. "Prospective Space Development." *Astronautics and Aeronautics* 10 (April 1972): 27.

Vonnegut, Kurt. *Between Time and Timbuktu*. New York: Delacorte Press, 1972.

———. "The Manned Missiles." In *The Norton Anthology of Short Fiction,* edited by R. V. Cassill. New York: Norton, 1978.

———. *The Sirens of Titan*. 1959. Reprint. New York: Delacorte Press, 1971.

———. *Slaughterhouse Five*. New York: Delacorte Press, 1969.

Weber, Max. *Economy and Society: An Outline of Interpretive Sociology*. Edited by Guenther Roth and Clauss Witlich, translated by Epharaim Fischoff et al. 3 vols. New York: Bedminster Press, 1969.

———. *On Charisma and Institution Building; Selected Papers*. Edited and with introduction by S. N. Eisenstadt. Chicago: University of Chicago Press, 1969.

Weber, Ronald. *Seeing Earth: Literary Responses to Space Exploration*. Athens: Ohio University Press, 1985.

Werge, Thomas. "An Apocalyptic Voyage: God, Satan and the American Tradition in Norman Mailer's *Of a Fire on the Moon*." In *America in Change*, edited by Ronald Weber. Notre Dame: University of Notre Dame Press, 1972.

Williams, Raymond. *Marxism and Literature*. Oxford: Oxford University Press, 1977.

Wolfe, Tom. "Columbus and the Moon." *New York Times*, July 20, 1979, p. 25.

————. Foreword to *Nine Lies About America*, by Arnold Beichman. New York: Library Press, 1972.

————. *The Kandy-Kolored Tangerine-Flake Streamline Baby*. New York: Farrar, Straus, and Giroux, 1965.

————. "The New Journalism." In *The New Journalism*, edited by Tom Wolfe and E. W. Johnson, 3–52. New York: Harper & Row, 1973.

————. "Post-Orbital Remorse: The Brotherhood of The Right Stuff." Four-part series in *Rolling Stone*, nos. 124, 126, 128, 130 (January 4, 18, February 15, March 1, 1973).

————. *The Right Stuff*. New York: Farrar, Straus, and Giroux, 1979.

Index

Aaron, Daniel, 147

Adams, Henry, 6, 77, 78

American West, 13, 20

Anderson, Chris, 83, 108

Apollo missions, 9, 115, 154, 155; *Apollo 11*, 9, 40, 48, 49, 52, 69, 71, 75, 115; *Apollo 10*, 27, 29; *Apollo 8*, 70, 156; *Apollo 12*, 70; *Apollo-Soyuz*, 145

Architecture, 9, 22, 31; and mass values, 72; high modernist, 77; as carceral space, 77, 83; as pastiche, 80; of cities, 97

Arendt, Hannah, 18, 33, 38, 40, 155; *The Human Condition*, 39; "Man's Conquest of Space," 40

Armstrong, Neil, 9

Astronauts, 6–15, 18, 43, 48, 54, 59, 64, 75, 81, 83, 86, 103–7, 116

Atomic bomb, 48

Bellow, Saul, 15–23, 97, 101, 114, 120, 145, 149, 154; *Mr. Sammler's Planet*, 15, 18, 29–44, 93, 100, 121

Brooks, Colette, 14

Bureaucracy, 18, 115; and charisma, 38, 129; rationality of, 82; language of, 83, 84; of mass values, 102; euphemism in, 134

Challenger, 6, 9, 100, 154

Charisma, routinization of, 101, 129

Cold War, 3, 7, 8, 14, 15, 100, 107, 123, 128, 150

Collins, Michael, 94, 96

Colonialism, 21, 35, 105, 125, 128, 134

Columbus, 13, 18, 50

Communications, 12, 22; global electronic, 8; mass, 9; and computers, 22; technology, 37; as industrial change, 62, 63

Cronkite, Walter, 5, 27

Cuban Missile Crisis, 5

DeLillo, Don, 17, 22; *Ratner's Star*, 15, 21, 90, 141–56

DeMott, Benjamin, 33

Disney, Walt, 27, 51

Dos Passos, John, 15

Eckhardt, Meister, 32, 42, 44
Eisenhower, Dwight D., 7, 20, 47, 124
Ellul, Jacques, 51
Emerson, Ralph Waldo, 14
Entropy, 127
Esquire, 134

Fallaci, Oriani, 100
Ferkiss, Victor, *Technological Man*, 18
Film: *2001: A Space Odyssey*, 48, 59,
    94; *True Grit*, 59; *Angel and the Bad
    Man*, 96; *High Noon*, 96; *Shane*, 97;
    Jeremiah Johnson, 98; *Die Frau im
    Mond*, 127
Fish, Stanley, 29
Fisher, Vardis, *Mountain Man*, 98
Frank, Pat, *Alas Babylon*, 5
Frontier, 7, 14

Glenn, John, 106
Goldstein, Laurence, 83

Hall, Edward T., 97
Heller, Joseph, *Catch 22*, 124
Hemingway, Ernest, 11
Herr, Michael, 134
High culture, 13
History, 10, 15, 23; centrifugal, 119;
    status of, 122; as parable of the
    present, 123; as socially mediated
    narrative, 124; power of "official,"
    125

Imperialism, 18
Intercontinental Ballistic Missiles
    (ICBM), 4, 10, 20, 120; "Missile
    Gap," 5; as classical allusion, 14–15
Intertextuality, 11, 56, 131

James, William, 8
Jameson, Fredric, 12
Johnson, Lyndon B., 51

Kennedy, Edward, 70, 71
Kennedy, John F., 7, 14, 51, 70, 141

LeClair, Tom, 148
Leitch, Vincent, 20
Lentricchia, Frank, 152
Life, 12, 40, 69, 70, 83, 103, 106, 108,
    112, 134
Literary journalism, 16, 101; as "New
    Journalism," 108
Lukács, Georg, 98, 123, 125
Lunar landing, 13, 19, 29, 51. *See also*
    Moon landing

Magritte, René, 72, 73, 85, 86, 89
Mailer, Norman, 8, 16, 21, 22, 33, 40,
    41, 100, 101, 108, 114, 120, 137, 145,
    149, 153, 154, 156; *Of a Fire on the
    Moon*, 15, 19, 69–89, 100, 119; *The
    Naked and the Dead*, 73, 78; *Armies
    of the Night*, 74, 82; *Why Are We in
    Vietnam?*, 134
Manichaeanism, 6, 17, 86, 87
Manned Space Program, 5–23 passim,
    51, 73, 74, 94, 104, 115
Manned Spacecraft Center, 76, 83
Manson, Charles, 70
Mazurek, Raymond, 124
McAuliffe, Christa, 9
McDougall, Walter, 6, 9, 10
Melville, Herman, 84, 85, 111
Mendelson, Edward, 129
Menzel, Donald, 33
Metadiscursive texts, 16

Milton, John, 29, 33
Modernism, 11, 12, 21, 32, 78, 90, 152; and urban environment, 144
Moon landing, 8–21 passim, 48, 61, 70, 81, 83; as technological achievement, 50. *See also* Lunar landing
Moonscape, 10
Moon shot, 10, 89
My Lai, 71

National Aeronautics and Space Administration (NASA), 7, 8, 10, 13, 21, 22, 51, 52, 59, 76, 79, 82, 83, 85, 86, 101, 103, 105, 111, 130, 141, 145
Newsday, 37
News media, 9, 11, 15, 16, 23, 50, 57, 71, 93, 103; mass imaging power of, 13, 16, 20; as postmodern spatial category, 54; commodification of, 55; as bureaucratic extension of NASA press office, 84; and celebrity, 101; image-making function of, 102; as mediated representation, 112; role of, 113, 114, 115; print and electronic, 60, 122
Newsweek, 12
Nixon, Richard M., 10, 51, 145

Paranoia, 13, 21, 27, 124, 131, 137, 142, 151; as "puritan reflex," 132; as plot, 147
Pastiche, 11, 13
Peterson, Bob, 71
Postmodernism, 7, 11–13, 17, 21, 22, 32, 54, 122; and hyperspace, 12; and culture, 22; and news media, 54; and decentering, 110, 111, 131; and historical fiction, 122

Power, 7, 16, 19, 29, 74, 129, 130, 134, 136, 144, 146; of technique, 35, 47, 55, 56, 61, 70, 73, 74, 119; architecture of, 77; as electronic systems, 78; of NASA, 84; as ideology, 86, 88; spaceflight as, 107; of military rank, 110; as protean force, 120; as zone of reference, 121; as grid, 124, 125; of multinational corporations, 126; of language, 128; of Vietnam memorial, 134; of historical narrative, 136
Project Apollo. *See* Apollo missions
Project Gemini, 8, 142
Project Mercury, 5, 8, 20, 38, 99, 104, 105, 110, 113, 114, 154
Puritanism, 18, 21, 30, 88, 94, 127, 132, 133
Pyle, Ernie, 11
Pynchon, Thomas, 17, 35, 73, 90, 101, 145, 148, 153; *Gravity's Rainbow*, 6, 15, 20, 21, 73, 101, 119–37, 145, 148, 151, 153; *The Crying of Lot 49*, 122, 124; *V*, 122

Rocket state, 6, 131, 148
Rockets, 6, 7, 19, 17, 143; German V-2, 4, 18, 122, 125, 127, 131
Roland, Alex, 145
Rolling Stone, 99, 101, 109
Rovit, Earl, 32

Sanders, Scott, 128
Shute, Nevil, *On the Beach*, 5
Sirhan, Sirhan B., 70
Smith, Michael, "Selling the Moon," 8
Social realism: in novels, 18, 32, 48, 93, 121

Soviet Union, 4, 20

Soyuz 5, 49

Space, 8, 12, 22, 30, 60, 70, 76, 122;
    race, 8, 135; program, 12–17 passim;
    conquest of, 15; interior, 65, 101;
    linear, 93; desert, 97; narrative, 109;
    domestic, 113; colonized, 127; as
    commodified time, 153; curved, 154;
    Archimedean point in, 155

Space Age, 6, 7, 15, 18, 21, 30, 31, 43,
    48, 51, 64, 70, 71, 100, 149;
    narratives of, 15, 23

Spatialization: of time, 15

Spectacle, 8, 10, 14, 87, 101, 114; and
    Debord's "Society of the Spectacle,"
    7; power as, 29; spaceflight as, 145,
    146; technological, 100, 101, 114;
    wartime death as, 125

Sputnik, 4, 20, 40, 105, 154

Stevens, Wallace, 13

Stonehill, Brian, 125

Taylor, Frederick, 11, 81

Technique, 51, 89, 90, 137, 144, 154

Technocracy, 7, 18, 49

Technocratic, 11, 19, 21, 62, 90, 132,
    144, 152; blandness, 72; culture of
    Space Age, 149

Technological achievement: of NASA,
    7, 8, 10, 13, 14, 16, 69, 70, 73, 75,
    87, 135

Television: imaging power of, 8, 9, 11,
    12, 14, 19, 31, 51, 54, 57, 61, 85, 134;
    as collective memory, 94; and
    creation of mass values, 150

Time, 12

Toffler, Alvin, *Future Shock*, 81

Tregaskis, Richard, 11

Turner, Fredrick Jackson, 14

Updike, John, 16, 48, 90, 93, 97, 101,
    114, 120, 145, 149, 154; *Rabbit Redux*,
    15, 18, 47–65, 93, 100, 121

Vehicle Assembly Building, 22, 76–81,
    83, 89

Vietnam, 9–19 passim, 33, 37, 38, 49,
    51, 57, 60, 62, 70, 74, 99, 122,
    134, 135

Von Bertalanffy, Ludvig, *General
    Systems Theory*, 148

Von Braun, Wernher, 15, 84

Vonnegut, Kurt, *Slaughterhouse
    Five*, 124

Webb, James E., 7, 8, 14, 130

Weber, Max, 18, 38, 101, 159n

Wells, H. G., 18, 30, 31, 34–36, 128

Whole Earth Catalogue, 156

Wolfe, Tom, 15, 16, 20, 22, 90, 101,
    120, 149, 154, 156; *The Right Stuff*,
    93–116; "Post-Orbital Remorse"
    series, 99; *The Electric Kool Aid Acid
    Test*, 108; *The Kandy-Kolored
    Tangerine-Flake Streamline Baby*,
    108; *The Pumphouse Gang*, 108

Woodstock, 71

World War II, 7, 17, 20–22, 48, 100,
    121, 123, 126, 128, 135

Yeager, Chuck, 20, 102, 115

Zone, 10, 106, 119, 128, 131, 133, 141,
    156; of history, 21; as fluid and
    boundary-less political space, 125; as
    depolarized space, 135–37